HAUNTED LIVERPOOL
CASEBOOK

© Tom Slemen 2010
Published by The Bluecoat Press, Liverpool
Book design by Michael March, Liverpool
Front cover illustration by Tim Webster
Printed by JF Print Limited

ISBN 9781904438953

HAUNTED LIVERPOOL
CASEBOOK

Tom Slemen

THE BLUECOAT PRESS

CONTENTS

TIMESLIPS

An inch of gold cannot buy a second of time. The most valuable thing in the world isn't gold, or platinum or diamonds, but time itself. For all his wealth, the richest man in the world on his deathbed cannot buy an extra second of 'life-time', yet we often talk of time as if it were a commodity: we speak of timeshares, of borrowing time, saving time, dividing our time, buying time and spending time. We even talk of killing time, but in reality, it is usually the other way round.

Once time is spent it is gone, and until we have the technology to control and reverse time, a moment spent is gone forever. Photographs and videos are two-dimensional forms of a bygone event, and they may aid our memory, acting as poignant souvenirs, as they give the impression that they have captured a moment, but all we are seeing is the image – we are not actually there. Some people occasionally dream of the past in such a way, they think they are actually back in their old childhood house, or with someone who has long since died, and however real these dreams may seem to be, they are but dreams.

The older we get, the more nostalgic we become, and the more we measure the values and situations of today by those of yesteryear. I know people who would like to establish an analogue society – a club where vinyl records are played, non-digital cameras are praised, and MP3s and other digital forms of entertainment are rejected as ersatz and inferior. We hanker after the past, and perhaps look at years gone by through the distorted rose-tinted lens of our mental telescopes, but even our ability to recollect from minutes ago is unreliable and poorly understood. If you show most people the following jumble of letters for ten seconds, and then remove this page from sight and ask them to recall or write down what they saw, only a few will be able to recollect the letters sequence: LEDIBMMOTITVIOUSOS

Though if I had written the letters in groups of three, as follows, it would have sunk into the memory a lot easier: LED IBM MOT ITV IOU SOS

And this is just a short-term memory test. When it comes to remembering incidents from yesterday, or a decade ago, or even further back, you will often find that two individuals will disagree about the details surrounding an event they both witnessed, but let's not get into the minefield of cognitive neuroscience, but agree that memories, even cherished ones, are often faulty. If it were only possible to go back in time, not through recollections, or by relying on photographs and videos, but by actually 'travelling' through time, just as the Time Traveller did in HG Wells's landmark novella of 1895, *The Time Machine*. Is such time-travelling technology possible? I believe it is.

In 1905 Albert Einstein published his Special Theory of Relativity, which predicted time dilation – the slowing down of time experienced by objects in motion relative to an observer. Then, in 1908, Einstein conjectured that gravity slows time as well, and by 1941, the time-dilation effect was observed to be a reality for the first time. Einstein and other freethinkers after him discovered that time was elastic – it could be stretched and even shrunk just by moving an object at high speed. This would have been unthinkable to scientists like Isaac Newton, one of the greatest scientists of all time, and yet Einstein was correct – time seems to tick away everywhere at the same rate. The clock in the bank says 4.10pm, and so the clock in the chemist must say the same, as must the time on your wristwatch, on your computer, or mobile phone – but if you synchronised your watch with the banker and the pharmacist's watch and then boarded a jet at John Lennon Airport and flew once round the world, you'd arrive home to find something peculiar (but not very exciting) had happened. The time on your watch would match the time displayed on the wristwatches worn by the chemist and the banker, but if their watches had a nanosecond display, you would discover that your watch was now 59 nanoseconds slower than their watches. A nanosecond is one billionth of a second. Because you moved faster than the stationary chemist and banker, time for you slowed down.

Okay, fifty-nine measly nanoseconds isn't a big deal, but if you boarded a UFO at John Lennon Airport, and it flew off at ninety-nine per cent the speed of light to a planet ten light years away in space, and then took another ten years to return to earth, how many years do you think would have passed during your trip? Well, for you, on board the UFO, the trip lasted less than three years, but for everyone else who was left behind in Liverpool, they would swear you had been gone for seventeen years, and they would all be seventeen years older than when you set out on your interstellar journey. Mind-boggling but true.

So, a time machine for travelling one-way into the

future would simply be a spaceship that could travel at relativistic speeds. If you wanted to travel to around 3010 from 2009, you would simply pull back on the throttle and travel in a vast circular trajectory at 99.99999 per cent the speed of light for six months. When you had completed the six-month journey, the clock would read 3010 AD.

That's all very well for travelling into the future, but how would you return to the past? Well, you wouldn't be able to do that with the spaceship. If you sped off for another six months at almost the speed of light, you'd simply end up in 4010 AD. To be a true time machine, the spaceship would have to allow us to travel backwards in time as well. So how about travelling into the past? This can be done several ways, but many of the methods involved are a bit too technical to go into here, so I'll just explain one of the more basic techniques.

You may not have heard of the physicist Willem Jacob van Stockum (1910-1944), but in 1937, he published an intriguing paper entitled, *The Gravitational Field of a Distribution of Particles Rotating about an Axis of Symmetry* in the Proceedings of the Royal Society of Edinburgh. Few men of science saw the implications of van Stockum's paper, but he was probably the first person to deduce the possibility of what are known as Closed Timelike Curves, which, in a nutshell suggest that a particle – and if the technology were available, a person – could travel backwards in time. Van Stockum said that time travel into the past was not only possible in principle, but was allowed by Einstein's equations.

The penny still hadn't dropped until the Austrian-American logician and mathematician Kurt Gödel (1906-1978) formulated another intriguing solution from Einstein's field equations in General Relativity. Gödel

9

discovered that if the universe was rotating (and most things in this universe are) then there would be paths, or orbits in space that a traveller could take to reach anywhere in space and time – be it in the past or the future. Einstein was disturbed by Gödel's mathematical model, and even had doubts about his own theories of relativity because of it. Rotation of massive bodies, long cylinders and vortexes of twisted space lie at the heart of the van Stockum and Gödel models, but physicists have also hypothesised other ways of travelling into the past involving seemingly far-fetched but real topological spacetime features such as wormholes, which could provide shortcuts through space and time, into the past or the future. These possibilities are not flights of fancy, but grounded in cold hard mathematical equations, and may one day soon provide the world with a way of travelling through time.

Perhaps in the meantime we should be looking towards nature to provide us with a key to timeslips, for there are some scientists and free spirited physicists who are looking to nature to see if she has already provided the conditions to allow what are known as 'timeslips', when people and places from the past or future are perceived by people in the present. The fascinating phenomenon of timeslips has been reported for centuries, and here is a case in point, gleaned from the *Leeds Mercury* of 18 July 1812.

Between 7pm and 8pm on the fine summer Sunday evening of 28 June 1812, forty-five-year-old farmer Anthony Jackson, and fifteen-year-old Martin Turner, the son of a neighbouring farmer, were inspecting cattle grazing at Haverah Park on the estate of Sir John Ingleby near Ripley, when the teenager suddenly noticed a very strange spectacle in the leafy distance. To the farmer he exclaimed, "Look, Anthony! What a quantity of beast!"

The farmer squinted at the bright spots a quarter of a mile away and realised they were not sheep or cows but foot soldiers in white military uniform, and in the midst of this unknown army there stood a man – "with a commanding aspect" – dressed in a contrasting scarlet uniform. The body of soldiers marched in perfect order to the summit of a hill, passing within one hundred yards of the farmer and the boy. After the soldiers had ascended the hill, another troop of men – this time dressed in dark military uniforms – arose from nowhere and went after the white-clad soldiers up the hill and joined them. Both parties then formed a letter L shape and had started marching down the other side of the hill, when suddenly, a large cloud of smoke obliterated the scene and reduced the visibility on the estate to such an extent, that Farmer Jackson and the boy Turner could no longer even make out the grazing cattle.

For two minutes, Jackson and Turner stumbled about in the limbo of the thick mist, until the teenager panicked and ran off, somehow finding his way home. The farmer and the lad were profoundly affected by the unearthly experience, but whilst the boy swore the whole incident lasted around five minutes, Jackson was adamant that it could not have lasted less than a quarter of an hour. It seems that each witness, then, had a differing perception of time, a phenomenon that is a recurring factor in timeslips.

The strangely-dressed soldiers seen by the farmer and the young farmhand have never been identified. However, closer to home, across Lancashire, Merseyside, Wirral, Cheshire and North Wales, there have been many timeslip incidents reported where witnesses were able to identify, or at least date, the people or places they glimpsed.

In May 2009, sixty-four-year-old Harry Waring of Little Sutton accompanied his wife on a shopping trip to Liverpool. During the excursion around the city centre, they visited the Albert Dock, the Liverpool One shopping and leisure centre, and finally browsed the shops of Bold Street, before catching the train home from Central Station. Whilst on Bold Street that afternoon, Harry experienced a 'funny turn'. He felt dizzy, and became disoriented. He looked around to find his wife was nowhere to be seen. His memory deserted him for a while and he had no idea who he was, where he was, or why he was on Bold Street. He saw a shop called Maternally Yours, which sold what looked like clothes and shawls for babies. In a daze he wandered into the premises of a travel agents called Arrowsmith Holidays Ltd. "What Street is this?" he asked a young man in Arrowsmiths, and received the reply, "Bold Street, sir."

Mr Waring walked out of the shop and his short-term memory gradually started to return. He noticed his wife walking towards him with a worried look, and she asked him where he had been. When he mentioned the funny turn, Mrs Waring took him to a cafe for a long sit down and a cuppa, and he was soon joking and back to his usual self. The amnesia episode was shrugged off as a bit of blood pressure trouble, but when Harry Waring later left the cafe, he could no longer find the shops he had seen earlier – Maternally Yours and Arrowsmiths the travel agent. A religious bookshop now stood where he had seen the baby clothes store, and further up the street stood the entrance to the Victorian Tea Rooms – but there wasn't a trace of Arrowsmith the travel agents, or the young employee who had spoken to Harry.

I later researched this incident and within the yellowing pages of an old trade directory I discovered that a shop called Maternally Yours (a supplier of baby linen) had once existed at 82 Bold Street – now the premises of a religious bookshop – in the mid-1960s, and during that same time period, Arrowsmith the travel agents, had existed next door to the baby linen shop at 80 Bold Street, now indeed the entrance to Jeff's clothes store and the Victorian Tea Rooms.

By what mechanism had a man in 2009 seen and entered shops that had existed some forty-plus years back in time? Mr Waring had never experienced a timeslip before and certainly isn't a man prone to flights of fancy. Did he physically travel back to the 1960s? or did his mind tune into the mind of someone forty-odd years away in time? It really is difficult to formulate a workable hypothesis, but it would seem that crossing the time-barrier is much easier and less dangerous than crossing the sound and light barriers.

In a timeslip, an entire district can somehow revert back to a previous age, though sometimes the shift in time may just single out a particular house, or even a single item. For example, one drizzly evening during the winter of 2004, a student who had lived in Liverpool for a few months, left his flat on Bold Place, which runs alongside St Luke's Church, and went to post a letter to a friend in Scotland. The letter never arrived, and so the friend in Edinburgh telephoned the student, asking if he had actually sent it. Assuming the letter had got lost in the post, the student set out to post him another letter, and walked towards the same post office pillar box he had used before – but it was no longer there.

The student had definitely posted the first letter into a pillar box at the foot of the steps leading to St Luke's Church, at the junction of Berry Street and Leece Street, but no signal red pillar box had stood on that spot for years. The student asked the postman, and he was categorically certain that, to his knowledge, no PO pillar box had ever existed at that junction. I researched the case, and located the pillar box in question – depicted in a Chambre Hardman photograph of St Luke's and upper Bold Street, taken in the late 1940s. The pillar box was gone by the 1970s, and certainly was no longer there in February 2004. The scenery and people around the anachronistic pillar box had all remained firmly rooted in the twenty-first century, and yet it would seem that the pillar box itself 'came through' from the past that evening. That letter never arrived at its destination and was never traced.

A similar postal timeslip occurred in May 1982 when Andy Connolly, a young man in his twenties, picked his morning mail up from the doormat at his home on Park Road North, Birkenhead. Among the usual bills and circulars there was a curious manila envelope which bore a rather unusual and startling stamp: it featured Adolf Hitler in profile. Across this bizarre stamp, the black-inked franking mark, which consisted of wavy lines, featured the German word 'Postzustellung' (which means service by mail) and was underlined by a swastika. The word 'Liverpool' was faintly stamped within the two concentric circles of the franking mark, along with the previous day's date. Thinking he was the victim of an elaborate joke, Andy opened the envelope and found that it was a handwritten letter from his friend John Hughes, who lived in Toxteth:

Dear Andy,

In three days I am being taken to a mine in Wales to dig for some ore they've found for the Island Station One power centre in Widnes. I'm not sure if they'll let me write from there. Tell Ojo I love her if you ever bump into her, and tell her everything was my fault and I wish I had listened to her.

They have removed nearly all the statues and the cenotaph in front of St George's Hall and someone said the statue of Wellington on the column will be replaced with a statue of Franz Freager. Lime Street is being renamed Goethe Strasse and the north-western internment camp is becoming really overcrowded with mezzies. They shot two of them here last week because they shielded a mezzy but you won't hear about it in the news.

If you don't hear from me for a long while don't think the worst, it'll probably be them stopping the mail again. Try jhgsAcorps as a last resort and get rid of this letter after you've read it just in case.

You've been a good friend for years Andy, and I hope I'll see you again in the Crib one day.

John

Andy later got in touch with John, who told him he certainly hadn't written the unsettling letter, and he had no idea who 'Ojo' was, nor what a 'mezzy' was, nor the whereabouts of the 'Crib'. The matter was never solved. Maybe – and it's a big maybe – for some brief instant in May 1982, the dimensions of our world overlapped the dimensions of a parallel word where history turned out very differently for Hitler and the Nazi party. Perhaps in that alternate world, Hitler decided not to attack Russia and successfully invaded the United Kingdom instead, and from that nightmare world, a letter intended for the alternate Andy Connolly, living on Island Station One, entered our familiar world.

The tabloid press runs stories from time to time about people receiving letters decades late, and the Royal Mail's postal system is usually the butt of these articles, with the usual reference to correspondence being lost down some 'black hole', or in a postal limbo, but in some cases perhaps such letters really do enter some kind of limbo; after all, many a true word is spoken in journalistic jest.

One late afternoon on Monday, 3 August 2009, at around 5.20pm, a bus, packed with passengers, was travelling up Wavertree Road, heading towards Picton Road and the Wavertree High Street. A number of passengers looking out of the left windows of the bus noticed some very strange things. First of all, the sunlight outside had rapidly dimmed and it was suddenly twilight. Some of the passengers also noticed what looked like gas lamps along Wavertree Road, and the Botanic Pub, which had been demolished, was not only standing, but was plainly lit up inside. Inside the Botanic Park, there were two cannon close to the entrance, and four of the passengers saw what looked like a mother and child strolling along one of the paths in old fashioned clothes. They both wore straw boaters.

One of the passengers, a Mrs McIver, said that during this apparent timeslip, she could no longer see the familiar white Art Deco Littlewoods building in the

Botanic Park. That imposing landmark has been standing there, overlooking the park, since 1938. Nor could any of the witnesses see the Wavertree Technology Park, but as soon as the bus reached the road that forms a bridge over the Edge Hill railway cuttings, the sun suddenly came out again, revealing once more both the Littlewoods building and Wavertree Technology Park. There once were Russian cannon, captured at Sebastopol during the Crimean War in 1855, placed in Wavertree Park as trophies, in Victorian times. These guns were later melted down for scrap during the Second World War.

A few months before that spectacular timeslip, children at the other end of Wavertree Road told their mother in Edge Hill that a "new shop" had opened called The North Pole, and they had even been inside it, but when the children went back to have another look, the shop was no longer there, replaced by a block of flats. Back in the 1970s, there was a joke-shop shop called The North Pole, run by a man who acted as a sort of secretary, or intermediary, for Santa Claus, and children would write their Christmas letters to him. This ghostly shop has been seen before, but why a shop that closed decades ago is reappearing again is a mystery.

Timeslips have been experienced by the most sober, trustworthy and rational people. Carl Jung, the famous Swiss psychiatrist, whose momentous work in psychiatry, dream-analysis, religion, art, anthropology, architecture, history and literature earned him several professorships at Zurich and Basel, experienced a timeslip that was backed by historical facts.

Jung visited the tomb of the Empress Galla Placida in Italy in 1933, and also paid a visit to the nearby church of San Giovanni. During his visit to the church, Jung was captivated by four stunning mosaics on the walls of the baptistery, which depicted sailing ships being tossed about by waves of exquisite blue and green nuances. Jung was a little baffled by the presence of the aesthetic mosaics, as he had been to the church before that year and had not noticed the four works of art on that occasion. In fact, he was sure there had been four windows set into that wall of the baptistry. He asked several people in the church if he could buy photographs of the mosaics but no one seemed to understand what he was talking about. Jung later asked a friend who was visiting that part of Italy to try and obtain photographs of the mosaics, but his friend said there were no mosaics where Jung had seen them – there were just four windows set into a drab-looking wall. Jung researched the background to this obvious timeslip and discovered that the Empress Galla Placida, who was entombed near the church, had decorated the walls of the baptistry with mosaics featuring the theme of maritime dangers after she had experienced a hazardous voyage across the sea – in the fifth century.

In the late autumn of 2002, Mike, a retired pilot, visited Liverpool to be with his mother on her deathbed at her home in Mossley Hill. After she passed away, Mike's brothers invited him to go to the pub with them, but the ex-pilot had no wish to drown his sorrows, his mother's death was too raw. Instead he set off by himself for a long afternoon walk, which took him to Calderstones Park. Pilots, like policemen, are trained observers, even when consumed by grief, as Mike was, and upon entering the park, he noticed a remarkable absence of fallen leaves, given the season, and he also noted a blanket of warm air that wafted towards him. He quickly stripped off his sheepskin coat and dabbed his forehead with a handkerchief as he strolled on through the park. Then he came upon a curious sight – a game of cricket in play. It was only then that he realised something was seriously amiss about all this. A pilot is constantly aware of the position of the sun, as it gives a basic sense of navigation, and the sun in these clear azure heavens was at its zenith – which meant it must be noonday. Yet Mike glanced at his watch, and the dial told him that the time was in fact 2.50pm.

This was not making sense at all, but he had still not realised that he had entered another time period, even after there came another, striking, clue that he was no longer in 2002. The vaguely familiar sound of a turboprop airliner buzzed overhead. Mike craned back his head, squinting in the actinic glare of the sun until he saw what he thought was a Cambrian Airways Vickers Viscount, a plane that had seen its heyday in the 1960s. Today it was mainly used in South Africa for making short hops carrying postal cargo. The quaint airliner slanted down to the south east, bound for John Lennon Airport.

Music was floating on the summer-like zephyr in the park. It was coming from a portable radio lying on the grass next to a group of young people who were lying or sitting in a group on the ground – watching the cricket. These people were dressed in the type of clothes Mike hadn't seen since the 1960s. Then he noticed the radio – it was the exact same model as one he had owned a long time ago – an Ekco portable, and Roger Miller's 'King of the Road' was gently drifting out of it. That song, Mike recalled, had been released around the mid-1960s. Only then did the revelation hit him – he had somehow strolled back to that period. His suspicions were

19

confirmed when he saw a vintage – yet pristine – grass-green Raleigh bike leaning up against a park bench, and on that bench a student was stretched out reading a paperback with his head resting on a rolled up pullover.

The lazy hum of a bumble bee, the soft embrace of the summer warmth, the sweet scent of freshly-mown grass, the distant clack of the leather clad cricket ball on the willow bat, and the nostalgic music from the radio, all blissfully combined to make Mike decide that if this was a timeslip of some sort, he would prefer to stay in that time. But equally, he somehow sensed that the scenery of thirty-odd years ago would soon vanish like the multi-coloured film of a soap bubble when it hit the ground. Over and over, like some meaningful mantra, he whispered to himself, "Please let me stay ... please let me stay."

His mobile phone started to ring in his coat pocket, and within a second the bleak chill of autumn 2002 returned. The cricketers had long gone, as had the student spectators and the music. Mike is not prone to hallucinations, and although it could be argued that he might have been under a lot of stress that day after the death of his mother, he was adamant that he had not been hankering after the halcyon days of his youth, but merely intending to enjoy a walk in the present. Instead, he had somehow stepped back into the past, possibly into the mid-1960s.

So what do all of these timeslips amount to? What do they hint at? When the sun sets, it is still out there in space, though it is hidden from our view until the next day, but we know it will rise again. Similarly, the past may seem to have gone forever once it has disappeared below the horizon of the current day, but just like the sun that has set, it is still there.

On 14 October 1947, a human being travelled faster than the speed of sound (which is 740mph) when Chuck Yeager broke the 'sound barrier' in the American X-1 rocket plane. For many years before that breakthrough, the idea of a person travelling faster than sound was not taken seriously by many scientists, but technically, long before 1947, people have been travelling even faster than the velocity of sound – even when standing still, relatively that is. You see, as you read these words, you and everyone else on this planet, are whizzing through space at eighteen miles per second as the earth circles around the sun in its great orbit. The sun is of course, also orbiting the Milky Way galaxy, but let's not complicate things. We don't ever sense the phenomenal speed at which the earth is travelling through space, and I believe that crossing from the present into the past (or future) is even easier and smoother than crossing the sound barrier, when the conditions are right.

What are these conditions? They could be the weather, a certain frame of mind, fluctuations in the earth's magnetic field ... There will be a breakthrough – probably sooner rather than later, the way our technology and understanding of the laws of nature are evolving. Only time will tell.

THE BLACK BUS

There are many strange tales, often dismissed as urban legends, that have been circulating in Liverpool for many years. I have collected most of these stories, a majority of them told to me by people young and old when I was growing up on Myrtle Street. The following is just one example, and I can't help feeling that there is more to this tale than a grain of salt.

A silver-tongued clock, somewhere in the depths of the night, was faintly chiming the arrival of midnight, when an explosive peal of November thunder tore apart the night air of Liverpool. The echoes of the deep rumble reflected back from the Wirral side of the river, and then all was still as the grave, but this was just the calm before the great hail storm. Crystal buckshot, born in mid-air, was blasted down from the heavens by the angry gales from the north. It clattered furiously against roof tiles and windows, and flicked the dying leaves from the hibernating trees like elfshot arrows from a faery sniper. The uncaring North Wind on high showered stinging hailstones down on to the short-lived mortals – into the smarting faces and raw hands of those unloved nomadic unfortunates who have only the sky for a roof. Bedraggled vagrants screwed up weather-beaten faces and hurried into sheltering doorways, and hedonistic night-revellers turned up collars and made a dash for clubs or taxis, the girls' screams blotted out by the storm.

At 2am the hail had gone – for now – and the city was being thoroughly rinsed by a Biblical downpour as a gaggle of homeward-bound clubbers gathered under the bus shelter outside the Mardi Gras nightclub on Mount Pleasant. Taxis were whistled for but failed to stop, but suddenly, a bus approached at that unearthly hour from the direction of the Shell station, coming from Lime Street. A 2am bus service was unheard of in 1966, but a young man, high on purple hearts, jokingly put his hand out – and to his great surprise the bus – bearing the number 12c – halted at the stop. This double-decker was painted black, its headlamps were of a faint gleaming amber, and the interior was in darkness, suggesting a drained battery, or the activation of some power-saving mode on behalf of the driver, but that driver smiled and beckoned the seven or eight people to climb on board his vehicle. How altruistic, but such kindness is typical of Liverpool people. The upper deck was already full, so the newly embarked passengers sat and stood downstairs, and chatted to one another while some lit up woodbines.

"Where's the inspector?" asked a bemused twenty-five-year-old named Ray, his inner ears still ringing from the music of the Mardi. Weighing up the situation, his fingers stroked his van dyke, as a blonde Twiggy lookalike seated opposite fidgeted with a loose false eyelash between her glances at him. Stu, the nineteen-year-old on purple hearts, was leaning on the pole at the back of the bus, callously waving at the drenched folk being left behind on Mount Pleasant. All of a sudden there was a flash of lightning, and hail began to pelt the bus. The number 12c accelerated at an incredible speed, and the inertia sent all those who had been standing, down on to the floor in a heap. Screams filled the vehicle.

Ray saw the Georgian doorways of Oxford Street flitting past the windows, and fear made him swear. "Slow down, will you?" he shouted towards the driver, but the engine continued its high-pitched whine and the bus careered on even faster through the driving rain. The Twiggy twin was quickly reduced to tears, and she clutched the arms of another young woman seated next to her. Abercromby Square whizzed by in a heart-stopping flash, and Stu was hanging from the pole, sick with fear. Ray estimated the bus's speed as being somewhere in excess of over 80mph at least, and still it was accelerating, throwing up tidal waves of rainwater as its tyres passed through puddle lakes.

What was that weird noise barely audible over the roaring engine? The passengers upstairs were all laughing hysterically.

"I'm getting off! I only live in the Bully!" shouted a bespectacled passenger, trying to convince himself that this was a normal bus. The vehicle tore up the hill of Grinfield Street, yet its engine didn't even labour one rev, and as the bus turned down Overton Street, it leaned sickeningly about 40 degrees to the right. Everyone on board thought his number was up as everything tilted, but miraculously the bus righted itself on the wrong side of the road and screeched into a curve which almost took it through the windows of Kay Nelson on Wavertree Road.

People prayed, cried and swore as the bus mounted the kerb of the Picton Clock traffic island and flew on down to Childwall. By now, they calculated that it was travelling at around 120mph and the petite blonde threw up all over Ray, as he edged to the back of the bus, wondering if he dared leap off the platform, where Stu was clinging on for dear life with his arms and legs wrapped around the bar and his eyes clenched shut. Ray wondered why the maniac driving the bus was going so fast, and how was he managing to do it – surely it was impossible for a double decker to reach such fantastic speeds. He suddenly felt a strange impulse to look up, and there on the shadowy stairs stood a pale-faced individual whom he immediately recognised – an individual who had been dead for over a decade – Mr Ryan, the dirty old man who had lived next door to Ray when he was a child. Ray found himself taking his late Nan's rosary beads from his inside pocket, and feeding them through his fingers as he recited the Lord's Prayer out loud. The middle-aged man who wanted to get off at the Bullring quickly joined in. It was obvious to Ray that this black bus, which could travel at speeds no corporation bus could ever attain, had something to do with the supernatural – the Devil himself perhaps? Ray suddenly had the sickening conviction that the passengers of the top deck were all dead people – and bad dead people at that.

"Thy kingdom come, Thy will be done!" Ray shouted, now directing the prayer at the silhouetted driver, and sure enough the bus started to slow down, finally coming to a halt on Childwall Valley Road. The passengers scrambled to disembark as quickly as they could, some shaking with fear and others with fury at having been subjected to such an ordeal. Stu tried to prise open the door of the bus driver's cab, intending to give him "a good pasting" but the vehicle's demonic engine began to throb as it stirred back into life and as a ghostly mist invaded the valley of Childwall, the black bus moved off, and in full view of the traumatised passengers from Mount Pleasant, the vehicle faded away into nothingness as it passed under the railway bridge that spanned the road.

GHOSTS OF THE CHILDREN'S HOSPITAL

On Thursday, 18 June 1970, ten-year-old Simon Smith was admitted to the Royal Liverpool Children's Hospital on Myrtle Street, suffering from severe stomach pains. Appendicitis was initially suspected but subsequently ruled out. A rare stomach bug was then thought to be the culprit and Simon was kept in the hospital for four days. On that first night away from his family, on a ward with several other children, Simon pined for his mum. He lay in his bed around midnight and watched the full moon beyond the windows, shining in the sky over Catharine Street. Its silvery radiance painted the wonderfully-kept 'Spanish Garden' next door to the Church of St Philip Neri with pearlescent ghostly light. Simon lay in his hospital bed surrounded by darkness and the unfamiliar cavernous ward as he gazed at the moon.

As he yearned to be with his mum, dad and two sisters at his home in Kensington, Simon Smith was startled out of his melancholic musings, as something flitted about on the face of the moon. The boy squinted at the ancient 'face' of the lunar orb; there was definitely some movement up there, and it scared him so much that he squeezed his eyes shut, and despite the dull persistent ache in his belly, somehow managed to retreat into the soothing world of therapeutic sleep – but his slumbers didn't last long.

At around 2.30am, the sound of children's laughter awakened him. Simon opened his weary, sticky eyelids and thought he was still dreaming, for standing before him was a barefoot boy in ragged clothes, with a flat cap on his head. He seemed to be around the same age as himself and he was surrounded by a halo of golden light. To the right of this spectacular apparition there was another radiant ghost – a lovable little glowing mongrel dog with a wagging tail. The children from the other beds in the ward were grouped around the golden vision, watching the unearthly duo with awestruck faces. The boy talked with a strange echoing Lancashire accent, and his words sounded like, "My name is Matty and my dog's named is Little Dunk."

The ghostly boy then cart-wheeled across the ward floor, pursued by his faithful little dog, until both vanished through a wall. There were gasps of amazement from all the children, but Simon noticed one child cowering under his bed, obviously afraid of the ghostly goings-on. The golden aura of the spectral boy and his dog still shone through the wall, and suddenly the two paranormal performers re-emerged from that wall. Matty threw his cap at the children, and it whizzed above their heads, curved like a boomerang, and returned to his hand. The children loved it. Matty, it seems, could even fly, but not Little Dunk, who comically hopped about and yapped at his airborne master as he flew about the ward for a minute or so. The levitating urchin swooped down on the children, who were in hysterics at his antics. Their laughter alerted a nurse, and just before she arrived, Matty told the other little patients "not to tell the grown-ups" about him, or he wouldn't be allowed to come back and visit them.

The strange visitations went on for three nights, until the boy who always hid under the bed – Malcolm – blabbed to a nurse about the ghost, which had perhaps been the shade of a child who had died in the old children's hospital. After that, Matty and Little Dunk never returned – but the children's hospital had other intriguing ghosts as well. A smiling woman in white was occasionally seen on the wards, always around 1am. Then, in the mid-1970s, a number of people witnessed a startling gaseous phantom in broad daylight, high over the hospital. One of the witnesses to this airborne spectre was twenty-nine-year-old woman Chrissy, who was visiting her child one warm May afternoon. Chrissy was walking up Cambridge Street towards the 'Children's' (as the hospital was affectionately known) when she happened to glance up at the towering hospital incinerator chimney, which was cream-coloured with an oval black top, so it resembled a giant spent match. Puffs of dark smoke began to erupt from the black head of the chimney, and one pall of dark vapour suddenly morphed into the form of a life-sized man with up-reaching arms.

Chrissy stood there open mouthed gazing skywards at the eerie well-defined figure, and several passers-by, noticing her spellbound by something in the sky, naturally followed her gaze. One of these was Gerald, a thirty-eight-year-old builder from Hope Street's Federation House. He had just been to see his pregnant wife at nearby Oxford Street Maternity Hospital, and he was heading for the Cambridge public house when he saw Chrissy and three other people looking up at the sky over the incinerator chimney. Gerald looked up and saw the uncanny figure of what seemed to be a man, devoid of any face, made entirely of smoke. As the builder watched, the man-shaped cloud twirled about like a ballet dancer performing a pirouette. The anomalous anthropomorphic vaporous being then travelled against the May breeze, flying through the blue skies towards the University clock tower on Brownlow Hill, where it was lost to sight. Just what the entity was will probably never be known. I'm not too sure what was burned in the incinerator next to the Children's Hospital, whether it was infected dressings, or whether diseased body parts from medical operations were also cremated there.

I have saved the best till last regarding the ghostly goings-on at the old Children's Hospital. In March 1968, there was an unofficial strike by Liverpool Corporation bus crews over a failure by the City Council to implement an already agreed twenty-three shilling pay rise. As a result of the strike, thousands of commuters had to walk home to the suburbs and just as many crowded the platforms of the train stations. No overtime was worked at the docks, and children were released early from school so they could get home at their usual time.

One of these children, who considered himself lucky being let out of his school at 3pm, was eleven-year-old Bobby. Instead of going straight home, Bobby left his school in south Liverpool and walked into the city centre, where he browsed the toys in Woolworths (and pocketed a few pick n'mix sweets) before paying a visit to Number 30 Moorfields – the address of The Wizard's Den, a joke shop, costumier, and purveyor of wigs, theatrical make-up, comical masks, party hats, false beards, party games, and books on sleight of hand magic. Bobby pressed his nose up against the shop's window and scanned the novelties and tricks on display: the Cut and restored Rope (one shilling and sixpence), the shilling Hindi Paper Folding Mystery, Goofy Teeth (ninepence), shilling Cigarette Sparklers, a Whizz Bang Pen (two shillings and eleven pence)...

Suddenly, someone grabbed Bobby by the arm and twisted it painfully up his back. He saw in the reflection of the Den's window that it was the dreaded school bully 'Bluetooth' – a nickname earned because of the appearance of one of his front teeth, which had a bluish tinge, where the enamel had worn away. Bluetooth rummaged in Bobby's pockets as he gripped the boy in an excruciating arm-lock. "Keep still or I'll break yer arm!" he threatened, and somehow, as Bobby tried to break free, Bluetooth exerted a little too much brute force – and he cried out in agony.

Bluetooth shoved the lad roughly across the pavement, where he fell to the ground and rolled out into the road – straight into the path of an oncoming car. The vigilant quick-thinking driver braked hard, but not before the front tyre of his car hit Bobby's shoulder, almost dislocating it. Bluetooth, followed by one of his cronies, ran off down Dale Street, then darted down Sweeting Street in a panic. Bobby staggered to his feet and started to cry, and a group of people quickly came to his aid, including the driver of the car that had hit him. He ended up in the Children's Hospital on Myrtle Street, where he was kept in for a week, mostly for observation, as his injuries amounted to little.

On his first night at the hospital, at around three in the morning, Bobby awoke. At first he thought he was in his own bedroom, but he remembered where he was when he saw the other beds illuminated by the faint light from the street lamps outside. He tried to get back to sleep, but couldn't. It started to rain outside, and Bobby watched the droplets of water splash against the window and trickle haphazardly down to the sill. Then he saw something which would haunt him for many years to come; an impossible sight, and he believed he was dreaming it at first.

Outside the windows, just above rooftop level, there hung a great sailing ship with eerie black sails. This ship hovered perilously close to the roof of the Philharmonic Hall, with its black sails billowing out in the rainy breeze, and as Bobby beheld the unnatural scene, he noticed that the floating vessel was gliding ever so slowly towards the hospital.

Expecting the flying ship to smash through the walls and windows of the ward at any minute, Bobby ducked under the blankets and braced himself for the impact – which never came. He heard echoing tapping sounds in the twilight ward, and when he emerged from under his blankets, he saw a terrifying figure walking towards the bed of one of the other sleeping children. The shadowy man's most striking feature was his large head of frizzy greyish hair, which sprouted out from under a close-fitting brimless cap of some sort. The tall gangly stranger – who was well over six feet in height – had a long hooked nose. He wore a dark sleeveless jerkin, white shirt with puffed out sleeves, and wide long trousers, the legs of which ran down to a pair of huge buckled shoes with thick soles, which clattered like heavy clogs as the weird figure moved about. Hanging from his waist was a sword, possibly in a scabbard.

There was no sign of the gravity-defying ship at this point. Peeping now over the edge of his hospital blanket, Bobby made a mental note that the profile of the eerie night visitor's face was just like the famous old puppet Punch. It seemed obvious to Bobby that the intruder had come from that ghostly black-sailed ship that had floated over the Philharmonic Hall a minute or so before. His attire certainly reminded him of those old illustrations of the Jack Tars of the eighteenth century – a buccaneer, or pirate perhaps.

The sinister seaman was stooping over the head of a sleeping child who was snoring lightly. His head was cocked to one side, as if he was listening to him, or perhaps checking to see if he really was asleep. He muttered something grumpily and then turned and walked towards Bobby's bed. Those heavy buckled shoes click-clacked across the scrubbed tiled floor of the ward. Bobby was so afraid, he ducked under the blankets and then slid sideways out of the other side of his bed. His hands reached down to the cold shiny floor, and he gently lowered himself down, trying to make as little noise and disturbance as possible, lest he be detected by the odd fellow. He crawled under the bed, shaking with fear, and watched as the enormous black wooden shoes with the big bright buckles halted just inches from his hand. He then heard a loud0 squawking sound, and the voice of what sounded like a parrot, letting loose a series of swear words and obscene phrases. The creepy maritime apparition answered this unseen bird, saying, "Hold your horses, will ye?" The parrot replied with a shriek and more foul language, the likes of which Bobby had only heard before from the lips of his uncle Jack. "Wherever be ye, yer marplot?" he asked, throwing back the blankets off Bobby's bed.

A huge green parrot with round red eyes flapped down on to the floor and cocked its head sideways so that it presented one of its demonic eyes at Bobby's startled face. "He's here, Luddy ... here belay!" it cried, and unfolded its long but tattered-looking wings.

Bobby found himself pelting across the ward without

any recollection of getting up from under that bed. He barged through the double doors and ran barefoot down the corridor, screaming at the top of his voice. The night nurse had to intercept the hysterical boy and calm him down. Breathlessly, Bobby told her about the black-sailed ship and the Punch-faced sailor with the devil parrot. It took a lot of convincing before Bobby finally accepted that he had suffered nothing more than a vivid nightmare, and after treating him to a mug of cocoa, the nurse escorted him back to his bed. "See?" she whispered, so as not to wake up the other children, "There's no pirate, or parrot here."

Bobby slept uneasily for the remainder of that night, and the ghastly big-nosed pirate and his foul-mouthed parrot kept appearing in his dreams, along with the ominous black-sailed ship. But on the following night, again at around 3am, he awoke – this time sweating from a nightmare in which the weird parrot had flown at him and viciously attacked him, pecking out his eyes. Rain driven by the March gales from the east pelted the windows, and Bobby, remembering what the nurse had said, decided to get out of bed and confront his fears head on. At visiting time he had told his mother and father about the ship he had seen, and the pirate and the parrot, and his dad had also reassured him that no ship could ever hover over the rooftops in that way – it was a physical impossibility. So, bolstered by everything he had been told, he crept quietly out of bed and tiptoed across the ward to look through the windows, which again were speckled and streaked with raindrops.

And there it was again! The ship was back, and this time its great bulk was hanging in the air with its nose tilted towards the roof of the Women's Hospital on

Catharine Street. Bobby took an unconscious step backwards, away from the window, recoiling at the terrifying sight looming in the skies above him. He turned and ran to the nearest bed, where a little blonde-haired boy was sleeping, and he roughly shook him awake. The boy let out a yelp and his eyes flew open.

"Look! Come and look at this, quick!" and Bobby pointed to the menacing brigantine, still tilted downwards over Catharine and Falkner Streets, as though it had just crested an enormous wave.

The little boy squinted at the window and said he couldn't see properly without his glasses.

"Well where are they then?" asked an annoyed Bobby, looking at the boy's bedside cabinet.

The boy reached out and opened a small door in the cabinet, took out his spectacles, and put them on with infuriating slowness. When he eventually got out of bed, he was pushed to the window by Bobby. The two children looked at the extraordinary baleful sailing ship suspended in the air, just a few hundred feet away.

"What is it?" asked the boy, whose name, Bobby later found out, was Jim.

"It's a ship, of course," answered Bobby, so relieved that Jim could see it too, "and there's this horrible ghost on it, and he's dressed like a pirate, and he has a talking parrot; they came in here last night, while everyone was asleep."

"In here? A ghost?" Jim queried with a distressed look on his round freckled face. "I've got to show Norman this," he said, and went to wake up his friend Norman and brought him to the window. All three lads had been watching the ship for a few minutes, when a terrifying drama began to be played out. From the darkened windows of the Women's Hospital, the ghost who had

34

entered the ward on the previous night was seen to rise up and was dragging behind him a grey-haired woman without a stitch of clothing on her naked body. He was pulling her up to the airborne ship. Her screams could clearly be heard, even above the loud clattering of rain on the windows, and the three boys watched in horror as the tiny figure wildly kicked her legs about as she was taken up into the shadowy vessel. Norman weakly suggested that they should go and fetch a nurse so she could call the police, but none of them moved, mesmerised by what they were witnessing.

Having taken on board its unwilling passenger, the ship slowly righted itself, raising its nose until it was horizontal. The main square sail of the vessel unfurled and, possibly catching the wind from the east, it moved off slowly towards the river. Within a few seconds it was lost to sight in the low rain clouds.

No one believed the children's story, of course, and Bobby was blamed for upsetting little Jim, who cried each night after that because he dreaded the return of the ship, and the nurses had great difficulty in restoring harmony to the ward.

That vessel was never seen again by Bobby after that night, but many years later, in the 1980s, he was visiting a relative in the Women's Hospital on Catharine Street, when he happened to glance out of the window at the old Children's Hospital, which was about to close down. His cousin Mike was also looking out of the window with him, and the two exchanged accounts of numerous childhood accidents and stays in various hospitals. Then Mike said something that knocked Bobby for six.

Apparently, Mike had spent a few weeks, during the summer of 1969, at the Children's Hospital, because of a gastric condition, and one night he had been awakened by two patients, both of a similar age to himself. They excitedly gabbled something about a ship sailing in the clouds outside. Sceptical, Mike went to look for himself, but only saw something indistinct pass across the disc of the full moon. The other children swore they had seen a ship, and one of the doctors on the ward even asked the two children to draw it with crayons, without looking at the other's work. To his surprise, the two sketches were practically identical. Later that week, Mike's father told him that there was a local rumour going round that a policeman on the Myrtle Street night-beat had also seen the same ghost ship flying down so low that it knocked a chimney stack off the Ear, Nose and Throat Hospital – next door to the Children's.

~

Many years ago, I heard a tale about the so-called Ship of the Dead, a legendary sailing vessel that comes down out of the clouds in port cities and collects the souls of sailors who are about to die and I once talked to an old merchant seaman named Williamson, who swore that he had seen such a ship when he was a child in the 1920s. He had been looking out of his attic bedroom when he saw the supernatural ship come down out of a bank of moonlit cloud, glide down over the King's Dock, and continue inland at chimney-pot level up Blundell Street. That street ran into Cornwallis Street, where his grandfather, who had been a sailor all his life, lay desperately ill. He had just been given the Last Rites when a strange wind whistled through the bedroom, and the old man smiled before peacefully passing away. The

Catholic priest and the dead man's three sons and two daughters all testified to having heard a wheezing accordion playing a sea-shanty, which became fainter and fainter over the course of a minute.

~

In 2002, a guard named Noel, who is now a born-again Christian, told me how, one night in 1998, he was working as a security officer on the night shift at a factory in north Liverpool. During his break at 3.30am, Noel went up on to the factory roof for a smoke and a cup of coffee. The panoramic view from the rooftop never failed to lift his spirits, and Noel took in the great expanse of the River Mersey sparkling in the light from a waning moon, with the lights of New Brighton straight ahead across the waters, and the empty vastness of Liverpool Bay to his right.

Something caught Noel's vision in the bay that night; a long rod-like object, black in colour, was sticking out of the waters of the Crosby Channel, and as the guard tried to focus on this silhouetted pole, a ghostly old-fashioned sailing ship emerged from the glittering moonlit waters. The pole he had first noticed had actually been the jib-boom on the bowsprit at the front of the vessel. Soon the triangular black flying, outer, and inner jib sails emerged, followed by the stem and the foremast. Foam sprayed out quite a distance from the surfacing ship, and for a moment, Noel imagined that he was witnessing the emergence of some kind of submarine, but when the sailing ship flew up into a short arc trajectory, and then belly-flopped back down with a dull splash, he saw the sails unfurl on the foremast, mainmast and mizzen-mast.

The ship ploughed on steadily towards the mouth of

the Mersey, and Noel switched on his walkie-talkie to summon two other guards – Sean and Jason – up on to the roof. The three of them watched the solid-looking, square-rigged ship scudding at a steady speed up the river until it was just a speck on the horizon. Noel later learned of another security guard at a Seaforth warehouse that the ship had been seen bursting up through the waves on several previous occasions during the 1970s. The name of the ship – which must have sunk long ago – is unknown, but many vessels from the eighteenth to the twentieth century, met their fate off the coast of Crosby and Bootle.

Could Noel's ship be the same as that seen by the boys in the Children's Hospital in the 1960s? And could it also be the very same one that was seen by the young Mr Williamson flying ashore in the 1920s? We will probably never know. Noel sensed something evil about the ghost-ship that night, and it proved to be the catalyst for a spiritual turning-point in his life, for soon afterwards he became a born-again Christian.

SUPERNATURAL COMPANY

A woman in her seventies, whom we shall call Anne, was sentenced to a miserable and lonely existence in a hi-rise tower-block in Cantril Farm around 1972. Her husband was dead and her selfish sons were all married and too preoccupied with their own lives to bother paying her regular visits. Anne had a morbid fear of the dark and had fed her electricity meter with four shillings on the bleak October evening when our story begins. The pensioner listlessly made her way over to the window of her flat on the fifteenth floor and looked out – for no particular reason, just that seeing other people, even from that great height, made her feel connected to the world outside.

She followed a hair-thin crescent moon sinking slowly through the purple dusk over West Derby on the western horizon and she yearned for some company to dispel the lonely hours as the clock on the sideboard ticked away with monotonous insistence. Although no windows were open, a wind from nowhere suddenly gusted through the flat, and a broadsheet copy of the *Liverpool Echo* blew off the dining table. As the indoor gale quickly subsided, a slight deliberate cough – 'ahem' – sounded just behind Anne. Had a burglar gained entrance to her flat? The truth turned out to be much more sinister. A fat-faced truncated man hovered in mid-air right in front of her. His body ended just below the belt line, where dangled a quivering glistening mass, which she took to be blood-smeared entrails. She passed out at the ghastly sight and when she came to she pulled herself to her feet using the arms of a chair, put on her coat, grabbed her purse and fled the flat. She pressed the elevator button several times in her panic to get away. I seemed to take an age before the lift finally arrived and she then rode down fifteen floors.

Having emerged into the cold night air, she wandered around in a daze, past a gang of children who jeered at her, until she reached Baron's Hey, where the pent-up fear inside her suddenly became too much and she burst into tears. It was then that she began to question herself. Had she really imagined that appalling man with no lower half, or had the constant soul-dulling isolation of her miserable existence finally turned her mind?

A silk handkerchief, scented with May blossom, was suddenly thrust into her hand, and Anne recoiled in shock. A tall dark man with a black moustache and a finely-tailored suit stood before her. A sympathetic half smile played on his lips and a kind pair of blue eyes met hers. In a well-spoken voice he introduced himself, saying his name was William and that he would be only too happy to escort Anne home to the hi-rise flats. Wary at first, Anne soon warmed to the suave middle-aged man, who seemed genuinely concerned about her. He accompanied her up to the fifteenth floor in the elevator and saw her safely to her door. She thanked him profusely, saying she did not know what she would have done if he had not come along just at that moment, then she bid him goodnight and went inside.

At half past midnight, just when Anne's pulse had returned to normal and she was thinking of making her way to bed, that icy mystifying wind returned once more, blasting through the living room, and heralding again the sudden appearance of the bisected man as Anne was in the kitchen making cocoa. She screamed, and backed away towards the sink, her hand frantically searching for a knife. Just as the half-man with his dripping entrails was about to enter the kitchen, William's debonair form suddenly materialised and intercepted the floating phantom by seizing its arm. Anne was now puzzled as well as frightened, and she watched in disbelief as the two figures argued and wrestled with one another until both of them vanished through a wall in the midst of the struggle.

William reappeared a minute later and beckoned Anne to come and join him in the living room. She eventually did so, and the man, who was obviously a ghost, told her to sit down. He explained how he was a 'spirit guide' and how the man with no legs who had terrorised her was the earthbound ghost of a nasty individual who had been cut in half in an horrific traffic accident on the nearby motorway a few years ago. He had somehow managed to crawl almost a quarter of a mile in that state, leaving a trail of blood on the tarmac and dragging his exposed entrails behind him.

William added that there were quite a few restless ghosts and lost souls in the area, and that, like moths, they tended to drift out of the darkness towards light sources at night. The spirits were mainly attracted to the lights of the flats in the Cantril Farm tower blocks, and those occupants who were psychically receptive were being spooked by them. This was all too much to take in and Anne felt faint. William brought her cocoa in and sat with her all through the night until dawn, when he suddenly announced that he would have to leave her.

Anne went over and over the night's extraordinary

events in her mind. She even considered putting herself into a home, but felt she wasn't really ready for that phase in her life yet, and so she resolved to stand her ground, and stand up to any supernatural intruder who might come to torment her. William was dead, she knew and accepted that, and yet she recognised his innate goodness, and believed that it should not be a barrier to a possible friendship with him, should he choose to come calling again. Indeed he did come calling, not just once but every night, and so Anne eventually became accustomed to William's visits, and as hair-raising as some of them were, she never felt lonely again.

HAUNTED HALLOWEEN

The last day of the old Celtic calendar was Halloween, a time when the ancient Celts believed that the·partition between the realm of the living and that of the dead was at its thinnest, when the dead could communicate with the living, and all sorts of supernatural activity could take place. Tradition holds that the spirits of the dead are allowed to visit their homes on Halloween, and the 'dark forces' of nature are at their height. The Druids of old observed Halloween, calling it Samhain (pronounced 'Sow wain' – which means 'end of summer') and no one but the Druidic priests was allowed to keep a fire alight during Halloween; all other lights were to remain extinguished at that time.

Fire was regarded by the Druids as sacred, and householders who required a flame had to pay the Druids a fee to put a holy flame on their domestic altars. Even the Romans observed Halloween, which they called Feralia, but celebrated it in February, at the end of the Roman year. Feralia, like the Celtic Halloween, was a time when the veil between the worlds of life and death was lifted, and the living acknowledged the dead with prayers and sacrifices. Here are three uncanny tales that took place at Halloween ...

On the Halloween night of 1977, at around 1.45am, at a house somewhere in Liverpool, fifteen-year-old Colin Whitlock and fourteen-year-old Joanne James, made harebrained preparations to run away and get married. Joanne's strict father, Eric, had caught his daughter and her boyfriend trying to elope once before, and he had a feeling they were about to try it again on this particular night, so he locked and bolted the front and back doors of the house. However, love laughs at locks, and Colin turned up at Joanne's house armed with a ladder. She lifted the sash of her bedroom window and kissed him, as he balanced perched on the ladder, then giggled with excitement. In the background, the old black and white television set was on, for Joanne hoped its noise would drown out any tell-tale sounds of the impending elopement.

"Hurry up," whispered Colin, gazing adoringly at his half-dressed sweetheart through the window. He had parked his dad's car in the street below, and was afraid of a policeman turning up any moment and catching them in the act.

"I'll be down in a minute ... you go on," Joanne told him, and then began to put on her tights. Colin remained at the window, ogling her naked legs. Giggling, she told him to go and drew the curtains. He climbed back down the ladder, just as Jo's dad knocked on the door, saying, "Are you talking to someone in there?"

Joanne turned the volume right down to mute on the television and angrily answered, "No! You're so suspicious you're hearing things! Leave me alone!" but her father opened the door to check on her. Then, satisfied that she was alone, went to bed. By now, the television channel was closing down, and a man appeared on the screen, probably a presenter, bidding viewers goodnight and reminding them to switch off their sets. The volume was still off, so Joanne couldn't hear what the presenter was saying, but she remembers thinking he looked quite attractive, though there was something about his eyes that gave her the impression that he was a pervert – she could spot them a mile off.

Joanne pulled up her tights, and as she did so, the eyes of the man on the television screen seemed to follow her hands as they adjusted the stockings up her legs. He then stared arrogantly at Joanne's stunned face and lasciviously ran his tongue around his lips and winked at her. Joanne threw her hands to her mouth in shock, and the screen darkened, but the weird presenter's half-lit face could still be seen smirking horribly at her.

Joanne let out a scream that sent her boyfriend Colin hurrying straight back up the ladder to her room. Unfortunately, just as the boy parted the curtains, Joanne's dad came rushing in.

"I thought so!" Mr James roared, through gritted teeth. "Caught you in the act, didn't I?"

Joanne mutely pointed to the face on the television, but it had now changed to that of a familiar presenter of the time, Charles Foster.

Mr James, when he finally cooled down, revealed a chilling explanation for the ghostly goings-on. Three years before on Halloween night, his friend Stuart Smithkey was about to go out for drink with his wife, when the girl babysitting their child complained that the television set was making an annoying buzzing sound. Mr Smithkey told his wife to go on ahead to the pub while he fixed it. Smithkey removed the set's back cover and accidentally electrocuted himself with the high-tension electricity supply of the television's cathode-ray tube. There were consistent rumours that Mr Smithkey had been having an affair with the sixteen-year-old babysitter just before his death. Joanne's thrifty father later fixed his deceased friend's television, despite its gruesome history, and proudly installed it in his daughter's room. Joanne was shown a photograph of Stuart Smithkey and it was the very face she had seen leering at her from the television set.

~

And now for another true Halloween tale. Around 12.45am one Monday morning in October 1966, a couple from Upton in their thirties – Roger Green and Cynthia Brookes – were returning home from their friend's house in Irby. As Roger drove his Ford Anglia along the stretch of Arrowe Park Road that passes the Landican Cemetery, Cynthia shuddered and said she had just felt a weird icy chill. She nervously cast her eyes over the passing nightscape, which was silvered by the full moon: the old riding school, the deserted golf course, a tennis court, Ivy Farm, the well-kept hedgerows, Arrowe Hospital (not yet called Arrowe Park Hospital), and the forest of gravestones in Landican on the other side of the road. Cynthia couldn't out fathom why, but she had a powerful sensation that there was something evil in the air on this night, but she said nothing about her strange hunch to Roger, as he was very sceptical regarding matters of the supernatural.

The Anglia took a left turn at the roundabout and travelled up the continuation of Arrowe Park Road. She estimated that it must have been almost 1am when something happened on this road that she can still barely bring herself to remember.

"I've never seen a moon so bright," remarked Roger, bending down to get a better look at the lunar disc through the windshield. "I bet I could drive without any headlights," and rather stupidly he switched the headlamps off.

"What're you doing?" asked Cynthia angrily and told him to switch the lights back on at once, reminding him that Upton Police Station was just up the road, but Roger just smirked and looked at the moonlit lane ahead. He could actually see quite a distance by the world's oldest night lamp. Cynthia turned her face away from him in disgust and looked sulkily out of the window at the dew-besprinkled playing fields. Roger was right, but she wouldn't admit it – the moon was unusually bright that night and it was almost like daytime outside.

"Hey what's that?" said Roger suddenly, pointing to a dark object in the middle of the road about two hundred yards away. It was black and heart-shaped with a white spot on the top and it also looked pretty tall. The pair of them couldn't work out what it was. It was blocking the road, whatever it was, and so Roger slowed down, and with the moon being so bright, he forgot to switch his headlights back on as they crept ever closer.

Then he let a profanity slip as he braked hard – not wanting to get any closer to the inhuman and evil-looking thing. They could now both clearly see that it was well over seven feet in height, had two huge folded wings, as black as the rest of its body, and it stood on two long pointed feet, but the most ghastly feature of the monstrosity was its head and face. The head – which was as white as snow – was that of a goat, but the face had a distinctly human-like quality with a grinning mouth and heavy-lidded eyes.

Roger's first impulse was to reverse the car, but he was in such a state that he stalled it. Cynthia screamed unhelpfully as he wrestled with the gear stick whilst stepping on the clutch pedal, making it even harder for him to control his panic. The goat-headed entity tilted its head down and grinned gleefully as it watched the couple's distress. With a grinding of gears the Ford Anglia suddenly jerked backwards and then reversed at high speed back down the road, away from the thing that was not of this earth. The car swerved wildly from side to side as it careered backwards down Pool Lane and then headed home via a long and winding route.

Throughout the journey, Roger kept on saying, "What was it? What the hell was it? Cynthia could find no answer but just kept looking over her shoulder in case the thing was pursuing them. At the time they were not aware that the same demonic creature had been seen earlier that week in the Childwall area of Liverpool and in November, just a few days after Guy Fawkes Night, it was seen by two walkers on Bidston Hill.

In early December, Cynthia's sister Maureen visited from her home in Merthyr Tydfil with her Welsh husband Dafyd. Roger, Cynthia, Maureen and Dafyd went for a drink in The Willows pub on Saughall Massie Road, and in the course of their conversation, the weird tale of their encounter in Arrowe Park Road came up. As Cynthia described the winged devil, the colour drained from Maureen's face. She and two other women had seen the very same creature on the night of Halloween five weeks back. They had been returning from a pub when they had seen the creature unfold its wings and soar silently into off into the heavens. One of the women believed it to be the Angel of Death, and that its presence had something to do with the recent Aberfan disaster, in which one hundred and forty-four people – one hundred and sixteen of them schoolchildren – had been killed by a landslide from a coal mining slag heap, which had destroyed houses and buried an entire school at Aberfan village, just a few miles south of Merthyr Tydfil. The incident was one of the major disasters of the twentieth century and around half of the survivors of the tragedy suffered post-traumatic stress symptoms for many years afterwards.

If the Angel of Death really did appear in the early hours of Halloween that year, what was it doing on Arrowe Park Road? Roger Green has admitted to me that he often sped down that same road on his way back from his friend's home in Irby, often when he had been drinking to his shame, and he feels that the horned abomination might have been some type of omen, warning him that he would die on that road, or kill others, unless he changed his ways. If that is the case, then perhaps death does sometimes give a warning.

~

I think most of us are familiar with the concept of the Guardian Angel, who stays with you throughout your life on earth, guiding you and shielding you from danger and harm. Some mediums believe most of us have spirit guides known as 'Doorkeepers' that stay with an individual from a time prior to birth, right through to the afterlife and beyond. Whether that is true I cannot say, but over the years I have collected many accounts of a mysterious benevolent force acting to prevent death and injury in people's lives, and here is just one of these intriguing cases.

On the night of Halloween, 1965, an unearthly mimic saved the life of a girl on Cornett Road, off Longmoor Lane, Aintree. Fourteen-year-old Mary attended Sherwood Lane Girls' Secondary Modern School, and after the 4 o'clock bell had signalled the end of the school day, she would almost always go to Hartley's newsagents for a bag of sweets before going home.

Mary's beauty soon caught the eye of fifteen-year-old Sam Miller of Inglis Road. He started waiting in the vicinity of the sweetshop and then following her home. He became so hopelessly besotted that he would often stand opposite the girl's home on Cornett Road in the evening and gaze, love-sick, up at her bedroom window, hoping to catch a glimpse of her silhouette on the lemon-coloured curtains. Three days into this stalking behaviour, infatuated Sam saw something that froze his blood. Just before 9pm, he saw Mary's silhouette come into view on the curtains and his pulse quickened. She seemed to be balancing on a chair for a few moments – then she dropped slightly and hung there, plainly suspended by a rope or cord. Her body was left swinging sideways, and Sam ran like fury across the road and hammered on her door until her father answered.

"Mary's hanged herself!" Sam shrieked. "You've got to save her!"

The girl's father was understandably taken aback by this remark. "Where?" he asked. "What are you talking about?"

"Up in her room! I've just seen her ... the curtains ... a rope ... I saw her fall off the chair. Please, please listen to me."

Mary's father looked down at the teenager with a puzzled expression.

"I don't know what you're on about, lad. She isn't in her room. Why, look, here she comes now!" he said, and looked past Sam down the road.

Sure enough, there was Mary walking towards her

50

house. She seemed preoccupied, as though she had something on her mind, and kept on looking over her shoulder, but she smiled and waved when she saw her dad, but who was that with him? It looked like Sam what's his name from school. What did he want? Sam backed away from the furious father and ran off without saying another word, and without daring to look Mary in the eye. How could he have made such a complete fool of himself in front of his beloved Mary?

Three days later, Mary was discovered trying to make a noose from a length of washing line in her bedroom. Then it all came pouring out – she intended to end it all, because she was being bullied by a local gang of girls and couldn't take it any more. Thankfully, her father had noticed her going upstairs with a length of washing line, and, recalling the chilling claim of Sam Miller earlier that week – a claim he had dismissed at the time as being just the imaginings of an infatuated youth – an alarm bell rang inside his head and he became suspicious and followed Mary up to her room.

His suspicions were immediately confirmed when he opened her bedroom door and found her standing on a chair fashioning the noose from the washing line. There was no other way of interpreting the scene which met his eyes. Mary, tears streaming down her face, fell into his arms and at last confided the deep unhappiness which had been gnawing away at her for many months and which she could no longer bear.

Mary had been saved by the eerie premonition of her attempted suicide that her admirer had seen three nights before. Mary soon learned of Sam's love for her and came to be very grateful for his part in saving her life. They started dating and three years later they were married.

GHOST IN BLUE

In October 1968, a sixty-three-year-old petty criminal whom we shall call Arthur, took Cathy, a girlfriend half his age, to an exotic meal at a Hawaiian restaurant on Toxteth's Upper Hill Street. "This used to be Dayawala the Chemist's place," Arthur recalled. He'd been 'away' for the last few years at Her Majesty's Pleasure, and pondered on the changes that had taken place in Liverpool since he'd done his time.

After the odd couple had ordered their meal, Cathy clasped Arthur's hand across the table. "Arthur, love, guess what? I want a baby."

Arthur was somewhat distracted, having been occupied making sly sidelong glances at the waiter, making a mental note of where he was going and what he was up to, imagining where the takings would be kept in a joint like this. Then it dawned on him what his girlfriend had just said, "A baby?"

Cathy nodded with a wide smile.

"What's the rush? I've only been with yer a month!" Babies were the last thing on Arthur's mind, but Cathy argued that they were not getting any younger; she was thirty-one and he would be sixty-four next December.

"I'm not sure. I'd need money, security, a proper house for me kid," Arthur said, pensively, but already filling with pride at the thought his as-of-yet unconceived child. "I haven't got a light. I'm in a tatty bedsit and your house is condemned. Not a great start for him. What could we offer a child, eh?"

"We could offer him … or her … love," Cathy replied, and we could get a job, and move to a proper house with a lovely garden up in Huyton.

"I'm on the NAB, love," said Arthur, with an air or defeatism, but he could see that Cathy was close to tears, and although he had gone through his chequered life pilfering anything he could get his hands on, regardless of the hurt he inflicted on others, he loved this girl, and it pained him to see her so disappointed. "Alright, love," he said, squeezing her little hand with his two big tattooed fists, "I'll sort something out, and get a few bob in."

Cathy still wasn't satisfied and wanted to know exactly how he was going to obtain the said 'few bob'.

Arthur's eyes darted shiftily left and right. "Well, I can't say that 'ere can I?" was his way of saying he'd be going on the rob.

"I don't want no tea-leafing, Arthur, I mean a proper job!" said Cathy, annoyed at his unspoken plans.

"God, girl, keep your voice down," he hissed through closed teeth, then leaned forward and said, "That fellah looks like a jack over there."

Cathy had finally had enough of his shenanigans. She got up from the table and flounced out into the misty evening. Arthur was too proud to go running after her, and left the restaurant after apologising to the waiter for cancelling the order. He went to the nearest pub, the Napier, downed three pints of black 'n tan, then wandered off to town, ending up legless outside Yates's Wine Lodge. His old friend 'Stanno' dragged him to a taxi and took him home to his house on Boaler Street, West Derby. During the cab ride, Arthur repeatedly said,

"What does she expect a man my age to do? Work for Cammel Laird?"

Stanno dumped Arthur, fully dressed, in the single bed in the spare room and left him to dry out. In the early hours, he was awakened by someone pulling the blankets off him. He swore at this mischievous nuisance and pulled them back on again, but the joker dragged the blankets off him again. Arthur opened his bleary bloodshot eyes and blinked, not quite believing what he was seeing – a bearded man in a policeman's uniform, surrounded by a faint blue glow, and whose face and hands were whiter than snow. His eyes seemed to be lit up with a peculiar golden radiance. Arthur was more than familiar with the modern attire of the twentieth century copper, after all, he had been involved with enough of them in his time, but this one's uniform was old-fashioned, like the ones in the old black and white silent films.

"I've done nowt, officer!" Arthur protested, more out of habit than unfounded guilt.

In what sounded like a rather quaint Lancashire accent, the backdated policeman stared directly at Arthur and issued him with an ultimatum: unless he went straight and returned to Cathy, who was a good woman, he would haunt him till the day he died.

Arthur let out a scream which brought Stanno rushing into the room. Stanno ran into the room but immediately halted and stood there, immobile, as he watched the policeman vanish before his eyes.

"Has he gone?" Arthur asked from beneath the blankets. "That creepy copper, has he gone, Stanno?"

"Yes," said Stanno, himself still stunned by the ghost's vanishing act. "Yeah, he did his vanishing act just as I came in."

Arthur took a peek over the blankets at Stanno. "Has he really gone?" His eyes flitted nervously about the darkened room. "So you definitely saw him as well?"

"I think so ... yes," replied Stanno, shaking his head in disbelief.

Arthur took the ghostly visitation very seriously and decided to heed its warning. From that day onward, he broke the habits of a lifetime by going straight and marrying Cathy. He later discovered a family secret – his grandfather had been a policeman, who had lived on Boaler Street in Victorian times – and by a strange quirk of fate, at Stanno's address.

By the way, a year after that creepy encounter, Arthur became a dad.

STRANGE VISIONS

When a vision is seen by just one person, it is usually explained away as an hallucination, or trick of the light, but visions seen simultaneously by a group of people, especially in broad daylight, are not as easy to explain away.

From 1997 to the present day I have been besieged with reports from people who have seen something very strange on the Liverpool waterfront – a mirage of a gigantic sculpture similar to the Statue of Liberty. One moment it's there, the next it's gone. Some have seen it as a fuzzy shimmering image, whereas others have seen it in great clarity. Some witnesses perceived the mystical statue as some kind of representation of Jesus, with his right fist raised in an uncharacteristic militant gesture, but the majority are convinced that it is a majestic-looking statue of John Lennon, with its right arm raised, and the hand gesturing the universal peace sign.

Inscribed on the four sides of the pedestal of the grandiose statue, a few witnesses claimed to have seen the words 'Give Peace A Chance' – possibly in various languages. Most of the reports of this ethereal statue place it somewhere facing the Raddison Hotel on the quayside of the Princes Dock, near the jetty.

I recently mentioned the visions of the 'Lennon Statue of Liberty' to Radio Merseyside's million-odd listeners via the *Billy Butler Show*. The response took me totally by surprise. I received almost a hundred emails and letters from people who had seen apparitions of the colossal airy white figure – and some had seen it as early as 1990. One listener named George, told me how, one summer morning in 1990, he and two friends had been trying to run an antenna wire between two blocks of flats in Birkenhead for their amateur pirate radio station, when they saw a huge white figure on the other side of the river, slowly emerging out of thin air, about four hundred yards to the left of the Royal Liver Building. "It looked like the Statue of Liberty, only she had trousers on," George recalled, "and my two colleagues also saw the it. Next thing, all we saw was seagulls again ... the statue had vanished."

In March 2009, Mr and Mrs Kay were walking their dog along the promenade at Seacombe, when they witnessed the gradual appearance of an enormous white statue on the Liverpool waterfront. Mr Kay happened to be carrying a pair of 8x30 binoculars around his neck, as he often enjoyed scanning the river in search of birdlife. He trained his binoculars on to the statue and saw that it was unmistakably a representation of John Lennon, standing in the same posture as the Statue of Liberty of New York Harbour, only instead of a torch being held aloft, the statue was gesturing with a peace sign, and the other hand had its fingers tucked into the left side-pocket of its jeans – quite unlike the hand of Liberty, which holds the tablet with the date of America's Independence inscribed upon it.

Mr Kay handed the binoculars to his wife, and she was able to make out even more details. Not only could she see the words 'Give Peace A Chance' engraved upon the river-facing side of the pedestal, she could also see buildings to the left and right of it that had not even been built yet, including a pyramidal structure that was huge, despite its distance in the morning mist, which partly obscured it. Mrs Kay could also see towers that would not have been out of place in the Manhattan skyline, because of their amazing height. St John's beacon, usually easily discernible with the naked eye, was not visible, yet the Liver Buildings were. As Mr Kay took another turn at looking at the incredible spectacle, the whole futuristic scene faded away to reveal the familiar Liverpool skyline once again.

What are we to make of these visions? Will a Fourth Grace of the Liverpool waterfront one day take the form of a pro-World Peace statue of Lennon, providing the city with yet another tourist attraction? Tomorrow will speak for itself.

~

Another vision, on a much smaller scale than the last, that of a robed woman in white, and said to have been the representation of the Blessed Virgin Mary, appeared on the back window of a house at Number 4 Tennyson Street, Bootle, in the 1940s. The window pane that featured the religious image was examined but no evidence of a hoax could be found, and pilgrims from across the country flocked to see for themselves the inspiring icon and gathered to pray in the backyard of the Bootle house, with many of the faithful reporting miraculous recoveries from a range of medical conditions. The image of the Virgin Mary eventually vanished as mysteriously as it had appeared.

~

A baffling possible shared 'vision' of sorts took place one afternoon in September 1974 when two black, colourfully-attired, turbaned jugglers arrived in Williamson Square to entertain the crowds of shoppers. They performed the famed Indian Rope Trick, selecting a ten-year-old child from the crowd to climb the rope – which was stretching about twenty feet into the air. The boy shinned halfway up the rope and then stopped, but was pushed up further by one of the exotic 'magicians' and after ascending a few feet, the second magician beat a drum loudly, and suddenly the boy had vanished.

The child's aunt was more than a little alarmed by his disappearance, and as the magicians collected coins from the astounded crowd, she summoned a policeman, who suspected that an abduction had taken place, disguised as some sleight-of-hand street act. The policeman quizzed the magicians, said to be Nigerians, about the missing boy's whereabouts and came close to arresting them for suspected abduction, when the missing child came around the corner of Tarleton Street around fifteen minutes later – unable to remember where he'd been.

One of the magicians smiled and told the policeman he had flowers in his helmet, and when the constable removed his hat he found two carnations inside, to the great amusement of the crowd. Moments later, the street performers were gone, but I have reports of them appearing in Toxteth around that time and performing similar mystifying acts of what seems like 'hypnotic' magic.

One Toxteth resident named Ian was fourteen at the time, and remembers one of the gaudily dressed men in a turban beheading a dog with a huge curved sword on Windsor Street. The canine head – with its tongue lolling out of the side of its mouth – was exhibited around the crowd of witnesses, many of whom were revolted by the decapitation and hurled racist insults at the men. A red and green satin cloth was then draped over the headless body of the dog, and the sliced-off head was placed under the cloth by one of the magicians as he muttered some esoteric-sounding words. The cloth was then whisked away, and the dog got up, shaking its head.

What is curious about the act is that several people standing some distance away could not see the dog's head in the hands of the magician as he was walking around the crowd. To them he seemed to be holding nothing at all. Hypnotic suggestion is often the last refuge of the sceptic, but in this case I suspect that something along the lines of mass hypnosis – perhaps telepathically broadcast into most of the minds of the people in the immediate circle around the show – was at work on that day.

Some visions are very difficult to explain and seem to defy our limited laws of 'common sense'. Here are just a few reports of some such inexplicable visions.

On 16 May 1980, dozens of motorists – including several from Merseyside – saw, of all things – a crocodile crossing the M55 motorway at Preston, and one motorist even ran over the out-of-place creature's tail. Police received so many reports about the crocodile, they searched the land on either side of the motorway for miles, but the creature was never found.

~

In the summer and autumn of 2006, dozens of motorists travelling along the M57 in the vicinity of Junction 6 in Knowsley saw a mirage of what looked like some enormous Bronze Age burial mound in the direction of Valley Road. Fifty-nine-year-old Maghull man Brian Petersen was one of the first people to contact me regarding the 'phantom barrow', as he described it. Brian was travelling from Prescot to Maghull one drizzly afternoon, around 4.30pm in June 2006, and as his vehicle approached Junction 6 of the M57, he saw a distant grey hill with a flattened top to his right, in the direction of Kirkby. "It was just like an ancient burial mound," Brian told me, "and I couldn't rationalise it. When I mentioned it to my wife Jenny, who was born in Knowsley, she told me that, many years ago, in the 1970s, a giant ski-slope had been built in Kirkby, and she marked an X where this slope was built on my A-Z street atlas – the exact spot where I had seen what I had perceived to be some kind of burial mound."

An artificial ski-slope, almost five hundred feet high, had indeed been built in Kirkby off Bewley Road and Valley Road in the mid-Seventies, at a cost of £114,000. The slope proved to be an utter disaster, as anyone skiing down it would have run straight into the perimeter fence that separated the slope from the motorway. This 'most expensive pile of dirt' – as the press called it – was also built over the major Liverpool to Kirkby water main, and was also a hazardous distraction to passing motorists. The slope was abandoned shortly afterwards, then levelled, and for many years, until 2007, there was nothing but a small grassy hill on the spot.

Bill Hampton, who saw the ghostly hill's silhouette one evening in September 2006 whilst travelling along Kirkby's Bewley Drive, now firmly believes that he was seeing some spectral image of the ski-slope from thirty-odd years before, and if that is the case, then this 'mirage' seems to be a timeslip. Bill saw the shadowy out-of-place hill silhouetted against the sunset, and even did a u-turn in his car to get a better look at it, but when he reached Valley Road, he found the hill was nowhere to be seen.

An off-duty policeman contacted me about his sighting of the Valley Road hill in early October 2006. He had seen the apparition on 21 July of that year at precisely 2.30pm as he drove his motorbike down Whitefield Drive. A trained observer, the policeman described the hill as around four hundred or so feet in height, with the circumference of the base about three hundred feet. There was a strange thin mist encircling the base, and when the police officer reached the traffic lights, about ten seconds after sighting the huge mound, he turned his head to find that the hill had vanished.

He never told anyone, not even his wife, about the peculiar 'illusion', as he called it, because he feared ridicule and believed his work colleagues would perhaps question his sanity. I was able to reassure him that others had seen the hill, and that, in all probability, it was some type of time-slippage centred on the old Kirkby ski-slope. This made him feel a lot better. So many strange and wonderful things have been seen by people who are afraid to tell others what they have witnessed, for fear of ridicule. It is my hope that through people reading my work, society will become more open-minded and receptive to the world of the unknown, and that people who have truly encountered things outside their everyday experience will not be called liars or regarded as cranks.

BLUE LIZZIE

Just days before the Christmas 1965, thirty-seven-year-old Jack Terry and his twenty-eight-year-old girlfriend Elsie Jones left the Knightsbridge Restaurant in Liverpool's Covent Garden and stepped into the stinging wintry night air. There was a visitation of pale sleet upon the damp cobbles of the poorly-lit lane, and Jack curled his arm around the smartly dressed Elsie as they headed towards Water Street.

Suddenly, a bluish radiance appeared, as if a neon sign had been switched on in one of the many dark niches of the lane. Then a glowing blue figure of a naked woman stepped out into Jack and Elsie's path, and at that precise moment a high-pitched bell was struck by someone nearby. Elsie stopped in her tracks and clutched the lapels of Jack's leather jacket. Jack also stopped, more stunned than worried at the sight of the glowing nude with flowing long grey hair and eerie-looking eyes. What was obviously some kind of ghost then let out a terrible shriek that chilled them to their souls. The woman ran straight at them and as Elsie yelped and tried to bury her face in Jack's chest, he pushed her aside and bravely stood in front of his beloved sweetheart to face the evil-looking spectre head on.

The face of the phosphorescent ghost contorted into a horrifying grimace of pure hatred, and she lunged at Jack with her hands held out like claws. Jack Terry screwed his eyes shut, hoping it was all some kind of bad dream, but then cried out as he felt ice-cold fingernails ripping down his face. When he opened his eyes, the terrifying apparition had vanished.

By this time, Elsie was hysterical, and as she and Jack hurried past Oriel Chambers and on to well-lit Water Street, she noticed the long livid red scratches that started on Jack's forehead and continued over his cheeks, right down to his chin. Horrified, Jack felt his face. The scratches stung and his hand was smeared with blood. He and Elsie rode a taxi to his home in Sunbury Road, Anfield, where Jack's mother treated the scratches. She assumed that they had had a fight and that Elsie had inflicted them. Jack was disgusted that she could even think such a thing, and he told her about the ghost and how it had flown at him. Mrs Terry thought he was making the whole thing up to protect Elsie and said she didn't believe him. This triggered a flaming row, which ended with Jack staying at Elsie's home that night in Mildmay Road, Norris Green.

On Christmas Day of that year, at around 5am, a policeman was walking past the Pig and Whistle public house on Covent Garden, when he saw a vagrant lying on his back in the middle of the icy road. Above him there was a faint smudge of light, but as the police constable looked on, he saw that the light was in fact a naked woman, unaccountably lit up, and she was leaning over the hobo.

"What's going on here?" shouted the policeman, upon which the woman instantly vanished.

Having been helped back on to his feet, the vagrant described how the ghastly ghost of the woman, who appeared to be about fifty years of age, had attacked him and knocked him to the ground. The constable did not know what to make of it, or how to record it without being humiliated by his colleagues, so he simply told the tramp to be on his way.

These attacks continued almost every year, always around Christmas time, and I researched the hauntings, only to make a chilling discovery. On Christmas Day, 1919, fifty-four-year-old prostitute Elizabeth McDermott, was strangled, stripped naked, and then mysteriously drained of every drop of blood on Liverpool's Covent Garden, just around the corner from the Town Hall. The killer, described by the coroner as an 'evil genius', was never caught, and for many years, always around the anniversary of her death, Lizzie McDermott's ghostly naked form, blue because it was devoid of blood, and with red eyes from blood vessels that had burst with strangulation, was seen prowling the area where she had been killed. Blue Lizzie may even walk again some night soon ...

GLASS ONION

Regular readers of my books will know that the concept of time is not as straightforward as it seems. The grammar we use to express our everyday thoughts has past and future tenses, and we talk of hours, minutes, seconds and days, but as of yet, no one is able to define exactly what time is, and it would seem that under certain conditions, everyday folk have walked into the past, and future, in what are known as 'timeslips'.

A reader named Roy contacted me early in 2010 to tell me of something that has haunted him for around forty-five years. In 1965, Roy was a frequent visitor to the world-famous Cavern Club on Mathew Street, and followed most of the acts appearing there, such as The Hideaways, and a beautiful girl known as Tiffany, formerly of the Liverbirds, who fronted a band called the Dimensions.

One evening, Roy went to see Tiffany and the Dimensions, and afterwards, he foolishly swallowed a dark-green pill that he had been given by a friend at a local pub. Roy was told the pill was a 'purple heart', the nickname of a drug consisting of a powerful combination of amphetamines and barbiturates, known medically as drinamyl, but for all he knew, it could have been anything. Roy suffered a panic attack fifteen minutes after taking this pill, and shoved his way through the crowds at the Cavern to get out and above ground, but when he staggered out into Mathew Street, twenty-two-year-old Roy saw it was daytime, which did not make sense. He could see that the street was unmistakably Mathew Street, but it was now pedestrianised and futuristic, especially the arcade of shops he staggered into. Roy was quick to notice that women on this unreal sunny day were dressed in a way that he perceived as provocative, even tarty, and in this strange arcade of chrome, glass, plastic, steel and neon, he felt very unsteady on his feet.

A girl of about twenty, whom Roy described as "an absolutely beautiful young blonde lady, with flawless skin and peculiar but fetching clothes", came out of a boutique of some sort and asked him if he was okay. The name of that boutique was 'Glass Onion'. At this point in time, the term Glass Onion, the title of a song John Lennon and Paul McCartney would later write for the Beatles' 1968 'White Album', was obviously unheard of.

As the girl came nearer and took hold of Roy's arm, he noticed two odd things about her; she had what we would now call a piercing in her lip, and a tribal tattoo on her hand. In Roy's era, tattooed women were the stuff of circuses and only ears were pierced. "Where am I?" Roy asked, before everything around him "dissolved into grey shapes" and he felt the ultramodern girl's grip on his arm lessen and then fade away.

Next, Roy found himself slumped against a warehouse wall on a bleak rain-slicked Mathew Street back in 1965, surrounded by a lot of people, all looking down at him. He passed out and woke up in the Royal Hospital, Pembroke Place, where he was kept under observation for a while. Roy confided in his brother and his closest friend about the tattooed blonde and the arcade which looked like something out of a *Dr Who* episode. "It must have been the purple heart," was his brother's explanation.

Roy later moved out of Liverpool and married a Surrey girl. He returned to the city in the late 1990s and on visiting the city centre was curious to revisit Mathew Street, the site of his strange experience. He was truly shocked to come upon Cavern Walks, and immediately recognised it as the highly futuristic arcade he had somehow visited back in 1965, but he failed to find a boutique called Glass Onion. Perhaps such a boutique will open there one day, and if so, will a young Roy make his appearance there?

THE CAP

In 2002, sixty-four-year-old Alan was working in his garden in Knotty Ash, when his wife Millie came out complaining of stomach pains. He only half listened to her because he was so absorbed in his work, saying she probably just had a bit of wind. Millie groaned, insisting that it didn't feel like wind at all, and that her stomach seemed to be bubbling. Whatever it was, she didn't feel well and decided to go and have a lie down. At tea time, ravenous from his day's gardening, Alan barged into the bedroom, asking where his tea was, but Millie lay there without answering. Her face was white, and she didn't seem to be breathing. The only part of her that seemed animated was her stomach, which was in turmoil. He could see it moving about and really did sound as if it was bubbling.

Alan shook his wife but there was no response and now all thoughts of his own stomach became irrelevant and he rushed to the phone to call an ambulance. The paramedics arrived within a very short time, but there was nothing they could do, other than break the news to Alan that Millie had died. A postmortem examination later revealed that she had died from a burst pancreas.

The shock of losing his wife of thirty years brought on a serious stroke, and Alan ended up in Broadgreen Hospital, semi-paralysed and slipping in and out of consciousness. He wasn't expected to live more than a week or two. All this took place just days before

Christmas. Alan woke up on Christmas morning to find his younger brother Philip sitting by his bedside, having come all the way up from Devon to pay him a visit. He brought grapes and a tonic wine and his wife came in carrying a huge bunch of flowers.

After he had exchanged greetings with his sick brother, Philip said, "Oh, look! What's this?" and showed Alan a Christmas present that somebody had left at the bottom of his bed. It was wrapped in cheap thin holly and ivy wrapping paper, and there was no card or label attached. Philip opened it for him and found that it was an old Liverpool Collegiate school cap, size six and seven eighths. Alan squinted at the cap and smiled lopsidedly, "That's my old school cap," he told his brother in a slow slurred voice, and he tried to reach out for it. Philip handed him the cap, and, after examining it carefully and scrutinising the badge on it, Alan recalled the motto of the Collegiate School in Shaw Street, which he had attended from 1949-1954: "Not Only the Intellect but also the Character," he muttered and again smiled. With his good hand, he managed to put the cap on his head, but his body immediately went into a violent spasm, then everything in the ward turned brilliant white, as if a searchlight had been trained on it.

Alan was no longer in Broadgreen, and Philip and his wife had gone. He found himself standing before his headmaster, Mr Croft, as a fifteen-year-old in the Liverpool Collegiate on Shaw Street. He felt younger, smaller, and lighter, and he looked around the headmaster's study and at Mr Croft who was talking down to him in a stern voice. Morning sunlight was streaming through the windows and he watched, fascinated, as small particles of dust danced in the sunbeam.

70

"Are you listening to me, boy?" came the stern voice. Then, without warning, Alan was back in the ward at Broadgreen. Having seen the drastic effect the cap had on his brother, Philip had removed it from his head.

"Put it back on!" Alan snarled, and his bewildered brother and wife exchanged puzzled glances, before Philip placed the cap back on his head.

Immediately, Alan found himself in the gymnasium with the PE instructor Mr Hanley supervising the class, as he and all the other boys did press-ups. Alan stopped exercising and looked to his right, and there was his best friend Jim, who would later die in the 1980s from a heart attack. And yet, here he was, in his early teens, all rosy cheeks and full of life.

"Jim, is that you?" Alan asked him. Jim smiled and looked sideways without stopping his push-ups. "Stop messing about, Al, or Tommy Hanley'll kick off," the boy replied.

Alan happily carried on with the press-ups and after the lesson was over, he talked at length to Jim, questioning him about the time and date, and Jim kept asking him if he was feeling alright. "No, I'm all confused, Jim," said Alan, and he ran off to explore all the old familiar classrooms and corridors of the Collegiate. He passed many familiar faces, including the English teacher, Mr Woodword, who told him to stop running. Then, without warning, Alan found himself back in the hospital ward once again. His brother and sister-in-law had gone, and a doctor was looking down at him with a bemused grin on his face. He was holding the Collegiate cap in his hands.

"That's my old cap!" Alan cried, and blindly grasped the air, reaching for it. He had already become addicted to the strange trips into the past and wanted more. The doctor believed the episodes were hallucinations due to the effect on the brain of the stroke, but Alan swore he was physically able to visit his old schooldays when he wore the cap.

As the weeks went by, Alan's condition improved in an unprecedented way. He told the specialists and doctors and nurses that the improvement was because of his old Collegiate cap, and a neurologist agreed that the cap seemed to be the catalyst for some sort of 'nostalgia therapy'. Within a month, Alan had regained the use of his left hand and leg, and he put it all down to the many days spent in the gym with Mr Hanley, his old PE teacher at the Collegiate. He also believed that the cap had somehow opened up a gateway into the past.

Unfortunately, however, on New Year's Day 2003, that old Collegiate cap literally vanished from the kitchen table in Alan's Knotty Ash home. They say laughter may be the best medicine, but nostalgia may be another cure-all remedy, and a journey into the past may be the best panacea of all, so if you're recovering from an illness, get out all those old photographs and start reminiscing!

WARNING FROM A WITCHWIFE

There comes a time when a girl feels she needs to step out into the big wide world and leave home. This is easier said than done in today's economic climate, and so many girls decide to share the financial burdens of modern life by moving into a flat with a friend, and this was exactly what twenty-year-old Gwen Harris did in the September of 1970, when she and a nineteen-year-old acquaintance, Mandy Perkins, moved into a two-bedroomed flat on Mount Street in the city centre, across the road from the College of Art. Both girls felt it was time to escape the stifling confines of their comfortable middle class lives. Mandy landed a job packing tea at the Kardomah Tea Merchants, whilst Gwen found part-time employment at a newsagents on Leece Street.

One afternoon at this shop, Gwen served a tall dark attractive man of about twenty-five, and as she handed him his change, he gently clasped her palm and remarked upon the softness of her hands. He then smiled and left. Later that day Gwen told Mandy about the sexy customer over a drink at The Swan pub on Wood Street, but her younger friend was too busy moaning about the smell of tea in her hair from working at the Kardomah and didn't really take in the information.

That weekend the girls went to the Babalou Club on Seel Street, and there Gwen again bumped into the man who had stroked her hand at the newsagents. He danced with her, told her his name was Robin, looked lovingly into her eyes ... and then introduced Gwen to his wife, Lyssia! Gwen had already been captivated by the man's charms and her heart wilted as she stood face to face with Lyssia, with her long straight black hair and dark green eyes set in a pretty porcelain-skinned face. Gwen was only too well aware of her own shortcomings – her red curly hair that would never do what she wanted it to and her freckles which covered her nose and cheeks – and believed she could never hope to compete with Robin's beautiful wife, even if she could get over the fact that it would be wrong to go out with a married man.

However, when the club closed, Lyssia stormed off after slapping Robin in the face, and he ended up embracing Gwen in a cul-de-sac at the top of Bold Street called Roscoe Place. Taking her face between his palms, Robin declared, somewhat poetically: "You for me, and I for thee and for none else; your face to mine, and your head turned away from all others." He explained that this was an ancient spell for lovers that no mortal could break. He made love to Gwen there and then in a doorway and she was powerless to resist.

When the girl got home she found a note from Mandy in the kitchen. She had gone home in a sulk because Gwen had abandoned her in the club to go off with Robin. But Gwen was now so besotted with Robin, that she never even gave Mandy a second thought. She thought of nothing but him and yearned for him to visit her as he had promised he would. On the following evening, at 11pm, an old woman came to the flat, calling out Gwen's name. Not sure what to make of it, Gwen opened the door, upon which the old crone issued her with a stark warning, "Have nothing to do with Robin!"

Having delivered this message, she then vanished.

Gwen slammed the door shut and stood there trembling, trying to make sense of the old woman's words. What could they mean? And how did she know where Gwen lived and that she had fallen for Robin? Three more times that night, Gwen was visited by the elderly 'ghost'. Her face appeared at the window on two separate occasions, silently watching her, and finally she appeared in the girl's bedroom. Gwen woke up paralysed at around 4am. The old hag's face stared deep into her eyes with her own peculiar faded green eyes. "I am Lyssia, Robin's wife, and he is older than me. I break the spell," she rasped and then recited a string of unintelligible words before vanishing.

Robin came into the newsagents the next day looking for Gwen, but she refused to serve him, and to protect herself she instinctively clutched a little crucifix that she wore on a chain around her neck. Robin sneered at her and stormed out of the shop.

It is said that Robin and his ghost wife Lyssia are still frequenting nightclubs in both Liverpool and London.

FRIGHT NIGHT

Even in this electronic age of Play Stations, Facebook and the Internet, there are children of a certain age who are still innocent enough to suspect that their toys may lead a secret life of their own after their parents have gone to bed. It is an old entrenched belief that apparently inanimate dolls may come to life when no one is around, but ludicrous as it may seem, sometimes they most definitely do.

What you and I term 'reality' is now classed by the new wave of psychologists as 'consensus reality' – merely an imperfect mental model, created by groups of flawed minds trying to understand how the universe works. I know people who scorn the idea of ghosts and the supernatural, yet check their horoscopes religiously in newspapers and magazines, and a priest who is a friend of mine could not accept the tale I am about to tell you, yet he believed that a statue of the Virgin Mary opened its eyes, smiled, and then blessed the startled congregation of a church in Ecuador some years ago.

The curtain of night had just fallen over Liverpool one unbearably humid evening in August 1857, and as the purple twilight gathered, the glow-worm gaslights of Lime Street's lampposts sputtered into life one by one, each jet ignited in turn by the lamplighter, as two young good-for-nothing dandies, with more money than sense, halted outside Allsop's Royal Waxworks, housed in the

Teutonic Hall, where the long-empty Forum Cinema now rots. Richard Evans and Jonathan Woosey, both aged twenty-one, and both born with silver spoons in their mouths, hatched ideas for outrageous dares outside Allsop's, where over a hundred wax figures, as large as life, of Emperors, Kings, Queens, Statesmen, murderers, hanging judges and execution victim, were exhibited.

Not so long ago the two young toffs had broken into Allsops to vandalise some of the wax replicas, leaving them posed in obscene positions. The wealthy fathers of the two privileged pranksters had managed to keep the case out of most of the newspapers on that occasion. Then there was the case of the old flower seller in Great Howard Street who dropped dead from fright when some irresponsible caped hoaxer with a painted red face jumped out on her dressed as Spring-Heeled Jack one evening. There were whispers around the fashionable clubs of town that the fatal scaremonger was Richard Evans, who had accepted a wager to kill a member of the fairer sex through the power of sheer terror.

Well, on this night the diabolical duo decided to raid the ghastly Anatomical Museum housed at the Freemason's Hall, opposite St George's Hall. Their perpetual high spirits further bolstered by absinthe and gin, the two jokers went to work just after midnight, sneaking from the moonlit Adelphi Hotel equipped with a glass-cutter and other tools of the burglar's trade, and within the hour they had entered Mr Emidy's Anatomy Museum, where a banner proclaimed, 'Man Know Thyself' stretching across a hall filled with four hundred and fifty detailed wax models depicting every disgusting infection, disease and medical condition that the organs of humans are heir to. This controversial exhibition, way ahead of its time, would go on to inspire Reynold's Waxworks and generate the dark germ of an idea for an equally infamous anatomical museum on Paradise Street. The idea was to steal a waxwork exhibit, preferably one of the 'opened' female torsos on display, and to send it in a parcel to a certain pompous reverend, whom Evans and Woosey jointly despised. Perhaps one of the life-like wax hearts could also be mailed to the police for "a bit of jolly", as Evans often remarked.

Woosey seized a replica of a diseased arm and became batsman in a grotesque game of cricket, with bladders and livers in turn bowled at him by an hysterical Evans. But the high-jinks was short-lived. A strange clicking sound suddenly echoed around the hall and two tall skeletons came strutting out of the shadows, both in perfect step like military men. They halted briefly, then chased after Evans and Woosey. Woosey pushed his friend aside in panic and escaped out of a window. Terrible screams rent the air, and when a policeman heard them and gained entry to the museum, he found Evans on his back, in a fit, frothing at the mouth, with a skeleton on top of him. Crimson crescents glistened on his cheek, the skull's teeth had apparently bitten him. Those two skeletons had been of young Russian soldiers shot by British troops at Sebastopol just a fortnight before. The bodies had been put in acid baths and the resulting skeletons had been sold to the museum of anatomy. There were dark rumours that the soldiers had been alive, but bound up, when they were placed in the baths, and had cursed the sinister doctor who turned their flesh and muscle into a sludge during the unimaginably agonising death by immersion in sulphuric acid.

Evans never recovered from the terrifying skeletal

attackers and ended his days shuttered away from society, dying one night as he screamed out in his sleep, most probably tormented by the vengeful ghosts of the Russian soldiers.

CHRISTMAS ANGEL OF DEATH

The Christmas of 1980 will be particularly remembered by some, because the world had just lost John Lennon, and, on a lighter note, it snowed that Christmas, and St Winifred's School Choir reached Number 1 with 'There's No One Quite Like Grandma' that day.

Upon the dark morning of that long-gone snowy December 25th, at 5.30am, as sleet and snow fell across the country, hard-working thirty-three-year-old security guard Sean was making preparations to leave the Paradise Street premises he had been patrolling through the lonely watches of the wintry night. As soon as 6am arrived, he would be off, and he intended to trudge northwards through the snow-carpeted streets of the city centre to his tiny flat above a shop on London Road. Then, after his seven hours of sleep, he would rise and watch a bit of telly to mock the same old Christmas Day films, as he munched his ready-made turkey dinner meal (cooked straight from the freezer). Then would come the real seasonal enjoyment – the poker game over in Manchester at a private club. Hopefully, the game would last into Boxing Day morning – the day when Sean would reach thirty-four years of age. Greenall Whitley, fine scotch whiskey, and a delicious cigar to champ on through the game – who could ask for more?

Sean returned to the cold present, and out beyond the snow-flecked windows, he saw a figure – an old woman lying face down in the snow. Sean was by nature very conscientious and would never leave his post for anything, but this was different. He didn't even remember running down the stairs and rushing out into the snowdrift that had built up behind the building. He lifted up the old woman; she was light as a feather, more bone than flesh. Her face was red-raw, her eyes were closed, and her hands, shrivelled like those of an ape, were bright scarlet, yet cold as the grave. The woman, who was aged around seventy-five, opened her bright blue eyes and suddenly whispered, "You're a good lad".

Within minutes, Sean had the woman, whose name was Mary, seated before his two-bar electric fire, with her hands around a mug of tea laced with rum. She claimed she was of Romany descent, a gypsy, and could read tea leaves with great accuracy, but this gift had caused some trouble in her family relationships and hence she had no one left now, and no real home to go to. Curious, Sean begged her to read his tea leaves, thinking it would be a bit of fun and Mary gladly agreed. But as soon as she took one look at the leaves clustered in the bottom of the cup, she seemed stunned, lost for words. Then came the warning, "Do not to travel by car over Christmastide." Sean was perturbed yet intrigued in equal measure, and he pressed the old woman for more information, till she suddenly told him something that would play on his mind: "There are many Angels of Death upon this earth, ready to take certain people away or warn them. In this area there is one named Angelystor, and if you take the journey you intend, he will collect you."

Mary insisted on leaving then, even though Sean had a list of questions he was dying to ask her, but, filled with the spirit of Christmas, perhaps, he gave her a tenner and bid her goodbye. She vanished into the whistling wind-whipped street amidst a new feathery downfall of snow.

When she had gone, Sean looked at the leaves in his teacup and was shocked to see the distinct numerals three and four – thirty-four – his age tomorrow!

It was 6am, time to leave, so Sean locked up the premises and threaded his way up Paradise Street, across Church Street, and on to Williamson Square. Not a living soul stirred and he took in the unsullied beauty of the scene. Coming along Roe Street, by the Royal Court, where a pedestrian bridge ran from St John's Precinct to Queen's Square, he saw, beneath this bridge in the darkness, a man, wearing a parka. "Got a light there mate?" came a Liverpool voice. Sean reached into his inside coat pocket, took out his lighter, and for the first time got a good look at the man's face. A grinning skull glared back at him from inside the parka hood; a skull with dice for eyes. One dice read '3' and the other '4' – there were those two numbers again. Sean ran off, unable even to speak, skidding on black ice as he crossed Lime Street, still afraid to look back.

The next day, his friend Tony arrived to give him a lift to Manchester but Sean refused to get in the car. For over twenty minutes Tony begged him to go with him, as they had planned. Eventually he lost his patience and swore at Sean saying, "What's up with you? We'd have been on the M62 by now! Stop mucking about, will you?"

Before he could answer, Tony's car, parked across the street, suddenly burst into flames. By the time the firemen arrived to put out the flames, the car was an empty shell. It was later discovered to have had an electrical fault that had ignited the fuel tank. Sean never gambled again, and he will never forget that Christmas when an unholy angel gave him a final warning.

IN A PICTURE

In the school summer holidays of 1977, thirteen-year-old Mick Butterworth from Dovecot went to stay with his Aunt Bridget over in Wirral for a week. Bridget owned a beautiful old white-painted bed and breakfast hotel on Parkgate promenade, which overlooked the silted up marshes of the Dee, and Mick loved staying with her, even though she seemed a bit stuck-up sometimes, and called him Michael instead of Mick like everyone else.

Anyway, that summer in 1977, Mick hadn't long arrived at his auntie's old Victorian house, when he started to feel ill. Whilst eating the full English breakfast, which he usually devoured with relish, Mick felt as if the bacon was made of barbed wire as it scoured its way down his throat, and by noon the doctor had been called out and had diagnosed acute tonsillitis. After the doctor had gone Bridget broke some bad news to Mick, "Michael, the doctor says your tonsils must come out when you're better." Mick immediately recalled the gruesome story his Uncle George had told him about that particular operation. George had woken up in agony after having his tonsils taken out, to find two nurses armed with toothbrushes desperately trying to scrub away the huge blood-clots in his throat.

Mick longed to go out into the seaside sunshine but instead Bridget took him up to a stuffy old spare room in the attic and put him to bed. The room, with its sloping

83

ceilings and dusty skylight window, seemed spooky, even during the daytime. The old bed, with its brass bed-knobs, felt slightly damp and smelt of old lavender. When Mick complained, Bridget told him he could always go home to convalesce if he wasn't happy, but Mick hated his overcrowded house in Dovecot, where he had no privacy and an older brother who bullied him. So he stayed put in the attic and hoped he would soon be well enough to go out and play on the sands of the Dee.

On the second day, in the afternoon, Mick was still very poorly but was sitting up in bed, reading comics and taking small sips of Lucozade, when he started to hallucinate with the fever of tonsillitis. There were three framed black and white photographs on the wall facing him, and one of these depicted three girls from long ago, possibly Edwardian or Victorian, wearing straw boaters and daintily holding up the ends of their long dresses as they stood barefoot in the shallow waters of a beach. Mick shuddered as he looked at these girls, because they were actually moving in the photograph, and the tide was lapping at their feet.

Then the photograph suddenly expanded and zoomed towards Mick, and he felt a sharp coastal wind on his face, and he found himself standing on that beach, and the three girls in old-fashioned clothes were pointing at him and giggling. He shuddered as he felt cold water creeping over his toes, and he jumped back away from the advancing tide. Then he noticed a huge sailing vessel leaning on its side in the sands. The beached ship had a hole in its barnacle-encrusted hull, and Mick stared into the blackness of this hole. Something was moving about in there. All of a sudden a wild-eyed man in rags with a shock of upright hair came running out of the hole with a huge knife in his hand, and he screamed like a lunatic as he plunged the knife into Mick's face. The teenager reflexively threw up his hands to protect his face and felt the cold blade glance off his wrist.

Everything in Mick's field of vision then shrank to a point of light, and he found himself once again sitting up in bed, sweating profusely. He tottered downstairs to tell Aunt Bridget what had happened, never expecting for a minute that she would believe him, but she told him a curious thing; the three girls in the photograph were Bridget's fifteen-year-old mother and her friends on Parkgate beach in 1902. There had been a wreck on that beach for many years, which an old hermit had made his home, and the local children used to taunt him, and he would chase them, sometimes drawing a knife as he did so. In the end the hermit walked out to sea one day and his body was never recovered.

On the following day, feeling a little stronger, Mick started mooching about in the attic and came across an old photograph album that had belonged to Bridget's late husband Frank, and one of the photos immediately caught Mick's eye – a picture of a young smartly-dressed Uncle Frank, with half of it torn away. He studied this photograph intently, and suddenly it seemed to expand and zoom towards him, just as the other picture had done. He found himself standing in some type of ballroom, and there was Uncle Frank, looking as if he were about twenty-five. Standing next to him was a beautiful red-haired woman of about eighteen. Now, the woman could plainly see Mick, but Frank apparently couldn't, and she kept staring at him very pointedly. Frank turned to the red-headed girl and said, "Nell, what's the matter? What're you looking at?"

Mick suddenly felt dizzy, and the whole ballroom became distorted, as if reflected in one of those trick mirrors in a fairground Hall of Mirrors. Mick's surroundings vanished to a tiny point, and he found himself in the bedroom once more. Again, he told his aunt all about the latest experience but got a reaction he had not expected; she was furious that he had been rifling through her private possessions. However, later on she softened and confided the real reason she was so touchy about that photograph. Apparently her late husband Frank, had once been married to a woman named Helen, but she had died from a heart condition only weeks after their wedding. In a fit of jealousy, Bridget had ripped the image of Helen, or Nelly, as she was nicknamed, from that photograph of her young husband.

Mick's 'metanormal' gift of somehow being able to psychically 'astral-project' himself into photographs, vanished along with his tonsillitis a fortnight later. Mick was surprised when I told him that other people had reported similar unexplained faculties to me over the years, that is projecting their mind into the past. Mick's brother Graham, a research chemist, could not accept my explanation, as he believed it to be too far fetched, but I reminded Graham how the entire edifice of science was based on some very shaky beliefs that were apparently more far-fetched than my conjectures. The Big Bang Theory, for example, accepted by most educated people today, hypothesises that the entire universe was the size of a pea 13.9 billion years ago! The specious present seems real enough, but that's just an illusion conjured up by the time-keeping suprachiasmatic nuclei in the brain, and they anchor our attention to this 'time period', but in reality, the methods and language we use to describe and measure the dimensions of time are meaningless. If you keep repeating any word, or even your name, over and over again to yourself, it becomes a meaningless sound and thought, and I strongly suspect that this revelation of seeing through the emptiness of the imagined present will one day lead to a mental form of time-travel.

GHOST WITH A GUITAR

In the 1960s and 1970s a whole neighbourhood between Prescot Street and Erskine Street – facing the Royal Teaching Hospital – was swept away by the bulldozers. In 1978, as the hospital was being built, a vast wasteground of rubble, consisting of the debris from all the demolished houses, became a poor child's playground. The locals called this desolate moonscape the 'Oller'.

Upon the Saturday of 31 December 1978, thirteen-year-old Franny Hardy left his home in nearby Paddington sometime after ten o'clock at night, and sought refuge in the deserted wasteground because his mother and father were fighting again. Franny always sought refuge in the Oller when he had no place else to go, and on this freezing night, he was cheered by the sight of a small welcoming fire burning in the middle of the wasteland. When he reached the fire, he saw a man he had never seen before sitting beside it in an old scuffed armchair with an acoustic guitar draped across his lap. Franny was a bit wary of the stranger, who looked to be in his forties. He had collar-length hair and his eyes were closed as he rested his chin on the neck of the guitar. Franny knew a few basic three-finger guitar chords, but he could see that the man was strumming far more complex ones as he hummed a tune that he recognised from years ago when his granddad was alive – 'Bad To Me' by Billy J Kramer and the Dakotas; a song which always reminded him of his late grandfather.

The guitarist opened his eyes and looked up at Franny without any expression of surprise.

"Cold, ain't it?" Franny said, by way of small talk, and he breathed out a cloud of condensed breath.

"Is it?" said the guitar-player cocking his head quizzically to one side, and Franny noted that he seemed to have no cloud of breath coming from his mouth.

Franny pulled up an old crate close to the fire and sat down. He asked the man if he was a tramp, but he shook his head.

"Well what're yer sittin' 'ere for then?"

"I used to live here," said the musician, his eyes scanning the no man's land of rubble that lay in the darkness beyond the fringes of the firelight.

"Where d'yer live now then?"

"I don't live anywhere," came the answer. "I died years ago."

The cold night air seeped into his Franny's bones, but he managed a false smile. "'ow can yer be dead if yer 'ere playin' a guitar?" he persisted, thinking the man must be joking – or more likely nuts.

"You'll know what I'm talking about one day," said the guitar-player, adding that he was now ready to pass over to the other world, as it had now been ten years since his death, and as his old house had been knocked down, there was no use hanging around anymore.

"Are yer really a ghost? Yer not messin?"

The easy conversation had reassured Franny and he was no longer scared. Anyone else would have been, but not Francis Hardy; his teacher even said his nervous system was wired up all wrong.

The man nodded, and began playing a beautiful soulful rendition of 'Auld Lang Syne'. As he played,

Franny coolly looked him up and down, trying to weigh him up, and when the piece finished, asked, "If yer really goin' tonight, can yer pass a message on to me granddad … Freddy Hardy?"

"If I can, I will. What's the message?"

"Can yer tell 'im I really miss 'im, and that me little sister Patricia still cries for 'im? Tell 'im … tell 'im I love 'im too," Franny added.

"At the stroke of midnight I'll be off, and it may take some time to find your granddad, but I promise I'll try."

"What's it like in the world yer goin' to?" Franny asked, picking up an old lolly-ice stick and tossing it into the flames of the fire.

"It's a beautiful place," said the ghost. "It's that lovely, few people want to come back, but I can't say much more, or they'll stop me from speaking. You'll find out for yourself one day."

Franny boasted that he had a good singing voice, but no one else thought he had, and his dad was always skitting him, saying he couldn't sing, so he did all his singing in the toilet.

"Go on then, let me hear you."

After coughing to clear his throat, and looking about in case anyone he knew was within earshot, Franny started to sing a song his granddad always used to sing – Frank Ifield's 'I Remember You'. The guitarist knew every chord and riff and accompanied Franny all the way through. The boy was delighted, as he had never been backed by a musician before. He asked the ghost if he knew 'World Without Love' – he did – and 'House of the Rising Sun', yes, that too and the beautiful sound of Franny's voice and the professional accompaniment of the acoustic guitar echoed across the expanses of ruin and desolation.

But then the music abruptly came to a halt. The horns on the Mersey sounded the arrival of midnight, and the distant cheers of drinkers swarming out of the pubs and out on to the streets to sing 'Auld Lang Syne' made Franny's heart sink.

The ghost stood up, quickly shook hands with Franny, then said, "I'm, sure we'll meet again one day. Goodbye, Franny."

Then he turned and walked away, leaving Franny cold, even though he was close to the fire, and choked up at his departure. He tried to shout, "Don't go", but the words couldn't escape from his throat and he had to watch helplessly as the guitar-man faded away.

Suddenly, a flash of light flitted over the side of Franny's face. It was the beam of a policeman's torch as he came over from his patrol car. Another officer followed him out of the car. They wanted to know the identity of the man with the guitar, and swept their torchlight around the dark wasteground in an attempt to locate him but he had vanished, even though there was nowhere he could have gone and no place he could have hidden. The policemen didn't know what to make of it and turned their attention to Franny. They told him that he had no business to be out at that late hour and to be off home at once.

That night Franny had a vivid dream in which his late grandfather appeared and said to him, "I received your message. I love you Franny and I'll see Patricia soon."

The next morning, Patricia told her big brother she had also dreamed of Grandad – or Gagga as she called him – and he had kissed her and held her.

Franny thought of the guitarist, and whispered, "Thanks".

THE DAY LIVERPOOL STOOD STILL

On Monday, 7 February 1972, thirty-year-old Catharine was travelling to her workplace in Liverpool University in the sidecar of a motorbike being driven by her husband Mike. There was a thick fog across the whole of the North West that day, and there was a terrible pile-up on the M6. In Britain, the weather rules all, of course, and so the authorities had warned people not to venture out by car unless their journey was absolutely necessary.

Well, Catharine had a mortgage to pay, and so she had no choice but to work, but she left her home in Aintree half an hour earlier than usual because of the fog, and at one point in the journey, as the motorcycle and sidecar were travelling along Walton Road, the fog became so dense, the red tail lights of the car in front were obliterated and all Catharine and Mike could see was a pale void of Limbo. The beam from the motorbike's headlamp was swallowed up by the choking fog, and Mike peered into his side mirror but could see nothing behind him but grey murk.

Unable to get his bearings and proceed safely, Mike pulled over for a while until the fog gradually started to thin. He could now just about make out the ghostly outline of nearby Lester Gardens and straight ahead was Kirkdale Road. At first everything looked as it should, but then as Mike kick-started the bike and drove on, the Bedford van in front of him wouldn't budge, and despite the appalling visibility, had no lights on. Then Catharine noticed a group of people standing on the pavement, and they were all stock-still like so many statues. It was the same with the traffic. Mike got off the bike and walked over to the driver's-side window of the Bedford van – the driver was staring straight ahead, as if in a trance. He had a lit cigarette in his mouth, with an inch of ash dangling precariously from the end. Mike rapped his gloved hand on the window but could get no reaction from him. When he looked down Kirkdale Vale and up Walton Road he saw the same eerie sight: buses, cars and lorries forming a convoy of stationary traffic, even though the traffic lights were on green to allow them through.

Catharine got out of the sidecar and stayed close to Mike throughout this sinister state of affairs. It was as if the whole world had come to a complete standstill, captured in time, just like a photograph. The fog thickened again, and Mike instinctively felt everything was going to return to normal, so he went back to his bike and sidecar and turned on the ignition. He revved the engine and suddenly there was a deafening sound of car horns and engines behind him as the whole cavalcade of vehicles started moving again in unison.

Mike was supposed to drop Catharine off near Senate House at the University but when he got there, they spent about fifteen minutes talking about the way everything had seemed to freeze in time. People naturally thought they were potty, but a man who worked as a surgeon at a local hospital later heard about the strange incident from a friend, and he said that on the same morning, he had been looking out of the windows of the Royal Hospital on Pembroke Place at the fogbound street, when he had noticed a very curious thing; the traffic had come to a

93

complete standstill – nothing unusual in that you might say – but then he saw a colleague on the pavement below who was on his way into the hospital. This man had a distinctive basin-cut hairstyle and bore a strong resemblance to the late actor Derek Nimmo, so there was no mistaking him. He was standing on the pavement with his left leg a few inches off the ground – in mid-step, as if he had been caught in a still photograph.

The surgeon opened the window and called to a group of people, pointing out the bizarre sight. The fog thinned and several other outlines and silhouettes of people – all stationary – could be seen across the road. Then suddenly, there was a burst of engine noise and the surgeon's friend outside ceased to be a flesh-and-blood statue and continued walking along as if nothing had happened. The surgeon and the group of witnesses later told the man what they had seen and he thought it was all a huge joke. He reported having felt nothing untoward as he walked towards the Royal Hospital.

I have collected quite a few examples of these time-freezes over the years, and they are usually highly localised incidents, happening within the immediate vicinity of the witness, but the aforementioned case is unusual, in that it was spread out over a few miles and experienced by more than one person.

HOUSE OF FEAR

On Wednesday, 1 May 2002, I entered the house of a friend who was on holiday, picked up his mail in the hallway, and placed it neatly in his letter rack. I was about to go and check all the rooms in the place and reset the burglar alarm, when I suddenly heard a radio burst into life in the living room. My friend's radio was incorporated into his midi system, and that was unplugged, yet a radio was blaring away in the corner, even though that particular corner was empty. That wall of the house did not adjoin any neighbouring house, for this property was detached and in a remote part of the greener Liverpool suburbs. As I carefully listened, I heard the distinctive voice of veteran DJ Jimmy Young. A vaguely familiar speeded-up voice I had not heard for years asked him, "What's the recipe for today, Jim?" And Jimmy Young in reply said something like, "Apricot and mincemeat pie, Raymondo."

I listened, intrigued, and later heard a sports bulletin about the state of play at Lords; Kent, with two first innings wickets in hand, had scored two hundred and ninety-seven runs against Middlesex. I also heard the sports reporter mention the English Captain Mike Denness, and soon realised that I was listening to a broadcast from way back, because Denness was at that time a cricket referee in his sixties. The transmission across time faded, and I subsequently discovered,

95

through research, that the cricket match at Lord's had taken place on Mayday 1975.

When my friend returned from holiday I told him about the strange aural timeslip, and he in turn told someone else, who related the incident to two amateur ghost-hunters, and they made the big mistake of trying to 'open up' the timeslip. These 'supernatural troubleshooters' (as they called themselves) discovered, through talking to the locals, that a man in his thirties had committed suicide at the house in question in the 1970s, by hanging himself from the banisters. This tragedy had taken place after the man, named Robert, had been abandoned by his girlfriend.

At the end of May my friend moved out of the house and went to live and work in North Wales, and the ghost hunters, Ian and Richard, squatted there, hoping to witness the reported paranormal phenomena. They heard the phantom radio, footsteps, male and female voices quarrelling up in one of the bedrooms, and the sounds of a man sobbing. Ian and Richard decided to stage a fake hanging, in the belief that if they performed a re-enactment of the suicide, Robert would be provoked into appearing. This crude conjuring act worked brilliantly – but at what a price! The rope was tied to the banister and the noose placed around Ian's neck. Another rope was tied about his waist with the other end tied to a stair-post on the first floor, to stop him from really hanging. All this was done at 1.20am – the time when Robert had reportedly taken his own life.

Minutes later, an inexplicable icy wind blew up from nowhere and whistled up the stairs, and then there came a tremendous hammering on the door that shook the house to its foundations. Richard went to the upstairs window to find a tall stocky man standing on the doorstep outside – and he had no face. There was an almighty crash in the hallway as the front door was knocked off its hinges by the unearthly late-night caller. Heavy footsteps came thudding up the stairs, and in panic, Ian struggled to free himself. He dashed upstairs and he and Richard retreated to a second floor bedroom. The terrifying figure burst in, grabbed Ian by the arm and flung him across the room at Richard, who was trying to escape out of a window. In the resulting impact, both young men went flying out of the second-floor window and plummeted over twenty feet to the garden below. Miraculously, Ian sustained no injuries but Richard sprained his wrist and chipped his front tooth on an overturned terracotta plant pot. The hapless duo of dabblers into the supernatural picked themselves up off the grass, looked in shock at the eerie blank-faced apparition surveying them from the upstairs window, then fled back to the safety of their own homes.

Undeterred, Ian and Richard were determined to get to the bottom of the uncanny goings-on in the house, and so they brought in a psychic whom they had tested with amazing results many times before, a pensioner named Margaret. She was not told about the violent ghost when she was taken to the house, at what they considered to be the safe hour of high-noon, but even in broad daylight, Margaret warned them that she detected an evil force that had been hiding in the house for over a hundred years, and it was actually watching the proceedings as she spoke. Ian asked Margaret if she knew the exact location of this evil force, and the elderly psychic said, "It's strange, this one, because I feel the house itself is … is somehow alive." Chillingly adding, "It's killed so many, by hanging, by cutting their throats ... even gassing and electrocuting some." The medium then put a handkerchief to her mouth, complained of nausea, and said she had to leave at once.

I undertook research into the house myself and unearthed some inexplicable and grisly mysteries associated with it. There had been a spate of strange suicides committed either at the house or just outside after the suicide had stayed at the house.

On the Tuesday afternoon of 22 August 1899, fifty-year-old George William Cornwall, a commercial traveller who had spent some time at the troubled house for reasons still unknown, had been found in a Chester and Runcorn railway carriage at Edge Hill Station with his throat cut so deeply, the blade had notched the spine – and yet the knife that took Cornwall's life was never found, despite an inch-by-inch search for miles along the train tracks leading to Edge Hill Railway Station. The coroner stated that the death had been a suicide, and a jury agreed with him at the inquest hearing, but the mysterious knife that had inflicted the 7-inch neck wound was never found. One surgeon said it would have been physically impossible for a man to cut through his own carotid artery, windpipe and food passage before discarding the knife out of the carriage window.

Ian, who was something of an electronics genius, used a red helium-neon laser, purchased from Maplin, to create a five-pointed pentacle star made from laser-light. He did this by fixing five one-inch-square mirrors to the walls and ceiling in the living room of the empty house with blu-tac and bouncing the red laser-beam around them. This glowing hi-tech pentacle was supposed to give them a measure of protection – but it had the opposite effect and seemed to provoke the wrath of the murderous paranormal entity.

At 8.30pm a voice could be heard, hypnotically whispering a certain obscene four-letter swear-word. Ian and Richard went in search of the source of the eerie voice, and established that it was coming from the cellar. With Maglite torches blazing, the investigators descended the cellar steps, and as they did so, the murmuring intensified. The bricks of the cellar wall were bulging in and out in the shape of a giant pair of pursed lips. Dust and debris fell from the cellar wall as the brick 'lips' whispered the profanity, and a rancid smell, mingled with the dank aroma of fungus, wafted towards Ian and Richard.

Then a black-handled dagger was thrust at the amateur investigators, but no hand was attached to the weapon. It simply hung in the air, and then lunged towards Ian's face, grazing his left cheek. Both men turned, and tripped over each other as they ran up the wooden steps leading out of the cellar in panic. Once they were in the hallway, they ran out of the house via the front door with the dagger chasing them for a while, and this time they never returned.

The house still lies empty. A psychic investigator who examined it in 2007 believes that the strata of quartz, sandstone and minerals that make up the bedrock of the house, act as an 'earth battery' – and the 'telluric' energy created by this geological generator via the house's copper and lead gas and water pipes (and electrical cables) is somehow responsible for the paranormal activity. That theory does not, in my opinion, explain what Margaret felt about the house, nor does it throw any light on the sinister 'mouth' in the cellar wall. The faceless entity which hurled Ian across the room and almost killed him, is allegedly still being seen, and seems to be some sort of sentinel, controlled by the evil force in the cellar of the troubled house.

A few years ago, a homeless young man who had taken shelter from the rain in that house, was awakened at four in the morning by screeching sounds, and when he opened his eyes and peered into the dark, he found the floor to be covered with a mass of writhing snakes. He sprang to his feet, and ran across the carpet of squirming creatures and out into the hall. He tried to open the door but the handle would not budge and felt ice-cold. A voice behind him called out his name repeatedly, and he heard footsteps coming down the hall towards him. A heavy cold hand touched his soldier, but at that same moment, he managed to yank open the door and run off into the night, leaving a haversack behind containing his belongings.

During research into the house of fear, I discovered that, in 1982, Amy, a girl of thirteen, used to meet a boy of her age near to the house in the evenings, and they were often seen embracing under a tree that stands about thirty feet from the haunted dwelling, which was empty at the time and in urgent need of renovation.

One autumn evening around 10.30pm, Amy was kissing her boyfriend, Adam, under the tree when she remembered that she had promised her mother to be home by 9.30pm, and so she told Adam she would have to leave pretty soon. Adam nodded and sighed, then looked up at the old vacant house, and what he saw there left him speechless. Amy noticed the awful expression on his face, and turned to see what was scaring him.

An uncanny-looking face was superimposed on the facade of the house. A pair of huge dark-rimmed eyes encircled each of the two upper windows, and the outline of a broken nose was visible in the front facade. Across the top of the door, a dark frowning mouth quivered. It was as if the eerie face was being projected on to the front of the house by something akin to a movie-projector, but as Amy and Adam looked on, they saw that the crooked nose was actually protruding, as if the bricks of the wall were bulging there. Adam turned and ran off, but Amy stood her ground, transfixed by the surreal vision.

"Amy!" The face on the house whispered the teenaged girl's name as a wind began to stir up a spiral of windswept leaves at her feet. Faint red light filtered through the 'eyes' formed by the two upper windows, lending a demonic aspect to the facade, and she suddenly had the irrational urge to run inside, even though at the same time she had a grim foreboding that she would die if she entered. A hand grabbed her arm. It was Adam, returned to pull her away from the sinister apparition, and he had to forcefully drag her all the way to her home, because she fought him every inch of the way, having an overpowering desire to enter the house and be destroyed by something. Amy was in tears when her mother answered the door, and understandably, she could not make head nor tail of the rambling account Adam gave regarding the house with an evil face.

~

Other strange faces appearing in the architecture of buildings have been reported to me occasionally over the years. I have received many letters and emails about the so-called 'Devil's Face' that could be detected in the bands of grey marble that were incorporated into part of the

Hexagon complex of the Strand shopping centre in Bootle. A reader named Marty, who played truant in his early teens, often hung out at the Strand, and during one of these afternoons of his misspent youth, he too noticed the huge sinister demonic face in the random bands of marble, and was suddenly overcome with a feeling of dread. As he ran away from the Strand, his heart began to thump and as he gasped for breath and dashed across Washington Parade, he was hit by a car. He was thrown a good few feet into the air by the impact, but miraculously suffered little injury besides a sprained wrist. He was convinced that the evil-looking face in the Hexagon had somehow jinxed him that day, and so he decided that never again would he risk looking at the image of the Devil in the Strand when he was in the shopping complex.

However, Marty's father was very dismissive of the whole thing, claiming there was no such thing as a face in the shopping centre. How could there be? It was just like seeing shapes of animals and people in the clouds, or a face on the moon. He was referring to the phenomenon known as 'pareidolia' where people see faces and other familiar patterns in jumbles of random images. The term also applies to 'hearing things' such as voices and music in white noise, such as the hissing sound of a shower or a waterfall.

However, months later, Marty's father's theory was put to the test when he visited the shopping centre with his son, who, sick of his father's scepticism, deliberately pointed out the Devil face in the Hexagon, and at that exact moment his father collapsed from a heart attack. Fortunately he received prompt medical attention and survived, but he never visited the shopping centre again and nor did Marty.

SECRET LOVE

The time: a sunny lunch-break in early May, 1964. The living tide of humanity flows on through the great thoroughfare of Mount Pleasant, 'each with their own secret cares' in a city which now finds itself the capital of the world, thanks to its four musical messiahs. A sweet scent of gloss paint hangs in the air, because two stump-smoking decorators are painting the railings of the YMCA, as their boredom-busting transistor radio plays 'World Without Love'.

For nearly a year now a young couple had been trying to make it to the Registry Office at 64 Mount Pleasant, but would always lose their nerve as they approached the Georgian town house. For the first time, nineteen-year-old Verity noticed the name of the furniture dealers next door to the potential marriage venue – the Wright Brothers. "Perhaps that's a sign the marriage will take off," she giggled, turning to Leslie, but the joke soared right over her lover's head. Only the previous week the couple had got this far, only to turn around at the last minute when they noticed a policeman crossing over from the direction of the Mardi Gras Club. Mind you, if he had found the forged birth certificate Leslie was carrying, who knows what legal consequences would have resulted?

Without knowing she was doing it, Verity began to hum the song playing on the painters' radio out of sheer nerves.

All she and Leslie had to do was go into the Registry Office, make an appointment with the Registrar, and then they could finally set the wheels in motion to live happily ever after as man and wife. They weren't criminals, after all, so why all the cloak and dagger schemes, just to legally solemnise the joining of two loving souls? Greedy demonic armament manufacturers across the world were, at that moment, spending billions on napalm bombs and automatic weapons to kill, disfigure and vaporise men, women, children and babies in Vietnam, and here were two innocent young people consumed by fear and guilt because they wanted to be married in a simple ceremony.

But the whole venture seemed to be jinxed, for now a man who knew Leslie from their schooldays was approaching, so the couple turned and disappeared into Roscoe Gardens, where they hid behind a monument, kissed and cried. One half of the couple was heartbroken. "Why are we even trying to be married? We'd need a witness anyway."

Leslie wiped away tears with a handkerchief, and Verity, the dreamer, agreed, "I know, it's daft, we may as well just live together." Then she told Leslie, "We're always saying let's pretend 'they' don't exist, but one day, even we won't exist. The trees will remember us and the moon. We'll come back as ghosts that no one can oppress any more, outside of this existence."

At that moment a gust of wind snatched the trilby from Leslie's head, and two male office workers, sitting in the gardens, soaking up a hazy sun in their lunch break, gasped. Leslie's beautiful long tresses, scraped back with pins, fell out.

"Flippin' 'eck! They're Judies!" laughed one of these white-collar observers.

The other swore, "Jesus! Were they necking just then?"

Leslie tried to put on the trilby but it was useless now, the illusion was flawed. The young women parted and sadly went their separate ways, Verity back to the shop where she worked, and Leslie, who had recently been sacked from a factory job, to her home off Berry Street.

Nearly a year later, in the spring, the couple were strolling together in Sefton Park when, without warning, Verity collapsed and died in Leslie's arms after a sudden and massive brain haemorrhage. Leslie couldn't face a world without love after a loss of such magnitude, and later took her own life.

I know that their ghosts still haunt the places where they had to hide their love away, and others have seen the often life-like apparitions of two young girls, hand in hand, walking through Roscoe Gardens, mostly in the springtime. The happy shades were spotted one evening by two guests from the nearby Shaftesbury Hotel as they skipped, carefree, holding hands, across Mount Pleasant, vanishing in the middle of the road. The ghostly duo occasionally even popped into Jack's Newsagents near Benson Street in 1982, where several students witnessed the girls vanishing into thin air after surveying the magazine racks.

Their union thwarted by prejudice during their lives, they now seem happily reunited in death.

THE KLEIDON

The sweet vermillion lips of autumn had caressed Liverpool at sunset, turning the ivory edifice of the Adelphi Hotel a lurid gold, and then, in the east, that ancient Queen of the Night we earthsiders know only as the moon, rose in her majestic fullness over Mount Pleasant.

In the meaningless reckoning of human time, this was the year 1974. The eternal stars came out one by one high over Lime Street as Mary Maidston, thirty-two-year-old kitchen assistant at the YMCA, left her place of work and stepped out on to Mount Pleasant. Her shoulder-length hair was honey-gold, thanks to 'Hint of a Tint' colour shampoo, and now, her greasy blue overall was rolled up with the rest of her belongings and stuffed in the small suitcase she carried, as she got ready to walk out on her husband and children.

She arrived at the rendezvous point, beneath the Dickie Lewis statue on Ranelagh Street, and there was Patrick, the man she was planning to live with for the rest of her life. A drunk from nearby Yates's Wine Lodge was giving a startlingly faithful rendition of the Billy Paul hit, 'Me and Mrs Jones' and the subject matter of the song cut too close to Mary's heart, so she urged Patrick to take her somewhere quiet. His blue eyes subtly suggested the Vines pub across the road. "No, somewhere quiet, I need to ..." Mary's voice trailed off and Patrick, at six feet and four inches, had to bend to listen. "You need to what?"

She shrugged, and hand-in-hand they walked down poorly lit Fairclough Street, behind Lewis's, ever mindful of someone seeing them together. They made their way, via back alleyways, stopping to kiss now and then, until they settled at the Roscoe Head, safely tucked away in narrow Roscoe Street. They sat there for nearly two hours, holding hands, preparing for the train journey to London, where Patrick was now renting a single bedroom flat. Mary had begged him to rent a place with rooms so her children could come and stay now and then, but Patrick said he couldn't afford it. It would be so hard living without her ten-year-old daughter Maureen and five-year-old son Jimmy. They were staying at their Nan's home for the night and she could picture them as her mother read them a bedtime story, all blissfully unaware that their mum was going away, and Mary's husband would not even be home yet. He was working the late-shift tonight.

"Are you sure you love me, Mary?" Patrick asked, clutching her hand.

"You know I do," was her subdued reply. She thought of the Enid Blyton books tucked away in her suitcase that Maureen had bought her, and she cried. Could she really leave her darling children? And what about her mum? What would she think? The time to leave came, and the rain fell.

"I'm not going!" Mary cried. "I can't, I just can't leave the children."

Ashen faced, Patrick told her, "If you really love me, you'll come with me."

But Mary's eyes filled with tears, and when they finally cleared he had gone. She got home just before her husband Phil arrived, and when he came in, the first

107

thing he said was, "That's funny! Look at your Enid Blyton books, they're all upside down in the bookshelf."

Mary felt so choked up at her unsuspecting husband's words, and she had to quickly use her cardigan to dab away a single tear that had escaped from her right eye. Then she hugged Phil.

"Oh, aye! What's all this then?" he said with a smile.

That night the couple made love and afterwards, Phil turned away from Mary and fell fast asleep in seconds. Mary lay wondering about Patrick, now somewhere in London, and the life with him she had renounced. She tried to drive all thoughts of him from her mind, but it was impossible, and she stifled her sobs, her face buried in the pillow. Then, suddenly, as the fingers of the bedside clock indicated four that morning, Phil grunted in his sleep, turned, and murmured, "I love you, Jill."

Mary Maidston's sorrow evaporated immediately, and now her mind was full of intrigue. Who was Jill? She racked her brains, and could only come up with Jill who lived across the road, a woman in her sixties. No, surely Phil couldn't be seeing her? Then, with a horrible sinking feeling in her stomach, Mary recalled the woman who had worked with Phil in his previous job at the travel agents a few years ago – a tall young redhead named Jill Horner. Phil had seemed pretty fond of her, and on one occasion – yes, Mary recalled it now, and what sense it made: that day when she was walking up Bold Street in a heavy shower, with rain like stair-rods; she had hurried to shelter in the doorway of a bank, and there were Phil and Jill Horner, standing unnecessesarily close to one another with looks of horrified surprise on their faces. Phil had gone to great lengths to distance himself from Jill, claiming he had not even noticed her standing there.

Then Mary suddenly remembered something Phil had said just the other day. He had asked her to dye her hair red; a coppery red – the same shade as Jill Horner's hair. And then there was Phil's old flame, Suzy McGregor. Why, she had been a redhead too ...

Phil started babbling again in his sleep: "I love, love, love, love, love you, Jilly!"

Mary slowly sat up, scrutinising her husband, trying her utmost not to wake him as she listened carefully for any more outbursts. Was his subconscious mind really revealing an affair, or was he just dreaming?

Suddenly, Phil's eyes opened, and with a look of apprehension, he turned to Mary and asked, "Was I talking in my sleep just then?"

"No," she replied flatly, coldly.

There was that indescribable look in his eyes that only a woman can interpret, and that look left Mary in no doubt that he was seeing Jill Horner behind her back. She decided there and then that she would leave Phil on Monday and travel to London after all, even though she had no real idea where Patrick had moved to in the capital.

Monday evening found Mary standing with her suitcase on the concourse at Euston Station, looking about her, as if by doing so she might find a clue as to Patrick's whereabouts. She walked out of the station into the thin-edged wind and wandered aimlessly through the handsome squares of Bloomsbury, feeling a complete fool. How on earth had she ever expected to find one man in a metropolis of millions? Still, she kindled an inner flame of optimism and held out against grim reality.

Mary visited a kiosk near the British Museum to buy a flat-tasting coffee and a red-striped box of twenty Embassy cigarettes, and then stood there in the cold heart of London, with her fingers wrapped around the warm paper cup as a fog blurred the edges of the urban landscape. Big Ben chimed the hour of nine in the clocktower of the House of Commons, and Mary drifted to the Victoria Embankment, where she smoked one cigarette after another, as the mist-enshrouded waters of the Thames swirled past her. Yes, she was geographically closer to Patrick now, yet paradoxically she felt emotionally light years away from her lover.

"Excuse me, but could I trouble you for a light?" came a sexless, feeble voice from behind, to Mary's left somewhere. It came from a woman in her seventies with a head of closely-cropped curly white hair and a wrinkled yet rather angelic face, despite the stub of a Havana cigar that was lodged between her shrunken lips. Mary rummaged in her handbag for a few moments and produced her trusty Ronson lighter. The old woman lit the remnant of the fine cigar and sucked away. Then she introduced herself as Hilary, and gave an unsolicited potted autobiography, telling how she had come to live on the streets of London. She had fallen into vagrancy after the death of her husband of forty-five years. She had promised him on his deathbed, almost ten years ago now, that she would shortly be joining him on the 'other side', by committing suicide, but after he died, Hilary found she couldn't fulfil her bleak promise and that broken promise had haunted her since.

Mary was deeply affected by her sombre tale, and she hugged Hilary. Then she told her about her own hopeless situation; how she loved Patrick, and had wanted to start a new life with him, but through a crisis of conscience had returned to her husband, only to find that he was having an affair. Now, she needed to find Patrick again,

110

but she didn't know where in London he might be, and felt such an idiot.

"Ah, you must never give up on love," Hilary assured her. "You must find him."

"That's easier said than done," Mary said, and sighed. "He could be anywhere."

There was a pause, and after a lengthy exhalation of cigar smoke, Hilary posed an odd question, "Do you believe in the supernatural, dear?"

Mary squinted through the acrid azure cigar smoke. "How do you mean?"

"Do you accept that there are forces at work in this world that are beyond our knowledge?"

"Well, I suppose there are ... why do you ask?" Mary was intrigued by the way the conversation was going.

"Have you ever heard of the Kleidon?" Hilary asked. Mary shook her head. "The Kleidon is a thing that gives answers to problems. It's a metaphysical entity, a force, if you like, that's there to help, if only you will look or listen."

Mary was impressed by the knowledgeable way she spoke, though her words meant little to her and she shot a blank look at the old woman as they stood there in the thickening fog.

"Look, to tune in to the Kleidon, you take a walk with a question constantly on your mind; naturally yours would be "Where is Patrick?" and then the first thing you hear will be the answer. You could hear it by switching a radio on and listening to the words of the disk-jockey, or maybe the lyrics of the song he is playing ... or it could come in the form of a snippet of conversation you overhear. The important thing is that you must be aware of the Kleidon, and then you will hear its answer."

Despite the intelligent way in which she spoke, it all

sounded like mumbo-jumbo to Mary, but Hilary's steely-blue eyes gazed at her with such intensity and seriousness, there was no doubting that she really believed in this Kleidon thing. Mary therefore felt obliged to at least try the mystical technique, but it was getting cold and her thoughts turned to the immediate question of finding shelter. She gazed at the river again, listening to the mud-coloured waters lazily lapping the walls of the Victoria Embankment, and her eyes wandered sideways to the eerie pointed obelisk of 'Cleopatra's Needle', which had been erected there in 1878. What force had driven men to carve out such a towering stone, in 1450 BC, and inscribe it with mysterious hieroglyphics? At the base of the needle were guardian sphinxes, the sight lending an altogether more sinister aspect to the scene in the ghostly fog.

Mary turned to talk to Hilary about the obelisk, but found she was no longer there. This startled her, and she hurried off, seeking a busier part of the city, fearing she had just been talking to a ghost. She made her way up Northumberland Avenue towards Trafalgar Square, and here Mary's heart raced when she thought she saw Patrick standing amongst a crowd of men near one of the Landseer Lions, but when she drew closer, and the figure turned round, she saw at once that it wasn't him.

In the midst of that crowded square, Mary Maidston felt so alone. She had come here with absolutely no strategy in mind. Then she remembered what Hilary had told her about the helpful Kleidon and how she should pose a question in her mind and keep it there until the Kleidon gave her a clue to the answer, which would come in the form of something overheard. So, with no other ideas forthcoming, in her mind's voice, Mary asked,

"Where is Patrick?" and then set off walking through the square, trying to listen in to conversations for clues, but there was so much background noise from the traffic, it was all just an indistinct hubbub of garbled sounds.

Then she noticed a busker with a guitar, and as she drew closer she realised that he was singing an old song by the Kinks, 'Waterloo Sunset'. Waterloo? Mary thought about the word – wasn't it a district down here in London? But where? And was all this just a load of nonsense anyway? The YMCA kitchen worker's mind was a hive of conflicting thoughts. She walked across the square towards the Strand, and here a curious thing happened, which seemed to be more than a coincidence. Mary was repeating the question in her head about her lost lover, when she noticed a piece of paper tumbling in the autumn breeze towards her. It was a fragment of the *Melody Maker*, and in bold print there was a word which struck a chord – 'Waterloo', in this case referring to the Abba song which had been released earlier that year.

This seemed to confirm that she should act on that name and she hurried to the first person she saw and asked them if they could direct her to Waterloo. A man told her to go down the Strand and turn right at the major junction at Lancaster Place. That led on to Waterloo Bridge. The man then asked her if she was looking for any particular place in Waterloo, but Mary shook her head, thanked him, and hurried off.

On Waterloo Bridge, Mary at first thought she was dreaming, for who should come walking towards her with his hands in his trouser pockets and his head bowed down towards the pavement but Patrick. He looked up and slowed his steps. "Mary!" he gasped, scarcely able to take in the fact she was there in flesh and blood. He had

113

been feeling depressed of late, and had decided to try and be positive and walk off his depression.

The couple lived together from then on at Patrick's little flat in Lambeth, and in the following year, Mary's husband Phil finally admitted he was having an affair, and Mary subsequently discovered that he had even been cheating on Jill Horner with a friend of hers. Divorce was the natural next step, after which Phil consented to the children living with Mary and Patrick down in London, as they planned to marry.

A strange thing happened on the wedding day that June, as Mary and Patrick left the church after being joined together as man and wife. Mary sat in the vintage car Patrick had hired for the big day, and as the vehicle moved away from the church, Mary spotted Hilary amongst the well-wishers, standing at the roadside with a knowing smile. She waved, and Mary tried to look back, but Patrick stopped her with a kiss. In her mind, Mary said, "Thanks, Hilary."

All the time, as we go about our daily lives, we overhear bits of songs, and snatches of conversation. All sorts of titbits of information greet our ears, and perhaps most of it holds no significance for us whatsoever, but just occasionally, if we listen really carefully, and take heed of what we hear, contained in those snippets might just lie the answers to life's problems.

RINGS OF POWER

The circle has no beginning or end, and is thus one of the ancient symbols of eternity, and this concept of eternity is embodied in the archetypal ring, worn to bond man and wife, ideally for eternity – or at least for the duration of one of their natural lives after the wedding service. The world's folklore is strewn with magical rings, and rings of power.

The wise King Solomon was said to have possessed a magical signet ring that enabled him to command demons to do what he wished and allowed him to talk the particular 'language' of any creature of the air, land or sea. The Norse God Odin had Draupnir, a golden arm-ring that reproduced copies of itself, and the great magician Merlin was said to have worn a magical finger ring, given to him by the mysterious enchantress Viviane – also known as the Lady of the Lake. Unfortunately, in Merlin's case, the ring's dark power took him over and forced him to fall into a false love with Viviane, which ultimately led to his downfall. Even earrings of a certain metal, if 'consecrated' by a witch, gypsy, or occultist, were thought to give increased powers of eyesight to those who wore them, and I have read many accounts of these earrings being worn by the Liverpool mariners of old.

In February 2008, excavations were being carried out for a new link road at Junction 6 of the M62 near Huyton, when workmen found over 3,000 objects dating back to the prehistoric age, as well as tiles and pottery that were made for the twentieth Roman Legion, which was based in Chester around 167 AD. Believe it or not, the archaeological site was deemed unimportant enough to delay the motorway scheme, and so the Highways Agency reburied it and it is now entombed in concrete and tarmac.

At that site up near Huyton and Tarbock, in the 1890s, sixty-one-year-old recluse, Valentine Gray, lived in a cottage with his wife of forty years, Anne. Gray had come into a fortune in his thirties and kept himself to himself. One day, a local farmer was ploughing his land when he unearthed something that glimmered in the soil. It turned out to be a rather crude golden ring, and the farmer showed it to Valentine Gray, who liked the look of it and suspected it might be very old, and purchased it for twenty-five guineas.

Gray had the ring examined by a respected jewellery expert, who told him it was a very rare object indeed; it was from the Bronze Age, and had been created about 1600 BC – perhaps much earlier. The jeweller had only ever seen one such ring before, unearthed in the Welsh hills when he was a boy. Mr Gray felt a strong impulse to wear the ancient ring on his wedding ring finger, and his wife Anna was in agreement; it was about time he wore a ring, as she had worn a wedding ring for four decades. Alas, Valentine Gray's personality changed overnight, and he soon discovered something very odd indeed: whilst ever that ring was on his finger, he could not tell a lie and life suddenly became very tricky.

One day his wife reminded him that it was his forty-first wedding anniversary, and she wheedled up to him and said, "Do you still love me, Valentine?"

"No," came the stark reply, "and for that matter, I never did love you either."

Mrs Gray was so taken back by his cruel disavowal, she burst into tears, and became quite ill from the shock of finding that her forty year marriage had been a sham. Valentine was normally such a caring man, and now he had changed beyond recognition. It was almost as if he was possessed. The Gray's physician, Dr Paul, had known the couple for most of their married life, and was surprised when they came to see him and told him of the problems they had been having. He listened to what they had to say and gently criticised Valentine for saying such hurtful wicked things to Mrs Gray. This sent Valentine into such a rage he almost came to blows with the doctor. Anne Gray was shocked and humiliated by his behaviour in front of the doctor and packed her bags as soon as they got home and moved in with her sister in Halewood village later that day.

News of Valentine's sudden and dramatic character change reached the ears of the vicar of the local church of St Nicholas, and he paid a visit to Valentine Grey and counselled him to repent to God for his wayward behaviour and to take back the dreadful things he had said to Anne. Far from being swayed by his words, Valentine told the Reverend that all the church wanted to do was take money off the parishioners and control their minds with "make-believe stories of Heaven and Hell". The Reverend was shocked, then furious, and he told Valentine the Devil was speaking through him, upon which Gray grabbed the glowing-tipped poker out of the fire and chased the sanctimonious church official out of his cottage.

Valentine was undressing that night, still seething with anger, when he took the ring off, and straight away he felt great remorse for what he had said to Anne and the vicar, and he started to cry. He suspected that the ring had something to do with his uncharacteristic behaviour, so he put it back on, just to see if it really was influencing his mind. Immediately he felt strong and ultra-humanly fortified, as if his blood had turned to iron, and once again he became brutally truthful. He soon discovered that, contrary to what the vicar preached, totally truthful people had to live in seclusion, as they offended everyone every time they opened their mouths.

A rather strange thing happened about a year later. Jane Leather, a dark-eyed girl of seventeen was illegally pulling up potatoes on land belonging to Foxhill Farm, when she unearthed a small golden ring. She placed it on the third finger of her left hand and a silly little fancy played in her mind; she pretended she was married, and all of a sudden she felt dizzy. Something struck her, which made her instantly recall how, when she was ten, a bolt of lightning had struck her cottage while she and her family had been sitting at the table for dinner. The bolt had struck the cast-iron fender round the fire, and a smaller snake of bright purple had flashed from the fender and touched the pewter bowl she had been holding. That terrifying tingling sensation she had experienced then was identical to the prickling feeling within her head this very moment.

She staggered towards a tree, and sat down at the base of it, shaking and was rather puzzled to find that she was now dressed in a long white robe. Beside her was a much older man with a grey beard, dressed in robes as white as Jane's. Her boyfriend, George Fleetwood, came to her aid, asked her if she was alright, and immediately spotted the gold ring on her finger. "What's that ring doing on your finger?" he asked, and reminded her she was promised to him.

"I don't love you," she told him, "and I will never marry you."

George then tried to remove the ring but Jane clawed at his face and bit him like a woman possessed. Her terrified boyfriend declared that she was a witch and stormed off. The tingling in Jane's head vanished, but, for some obscure reason, she then went missing from her home, wandering off in the middle of a raging thunderstorm. Who should find her in the same hour, soaked to the skin, sheltering under a hedge, but Valentine Gray? He brought Jane into his cottage, gave her food and drink, and dressed her in some of his wife's old clothes. He noticed the ring, and thought it resembled the one that had somehow exerted such a terrible influence over his own life. He persuaded Jane to go with him to the knowledgeable jeweller, who confirmed that the smaller ring was also from the Bronze Age, and probably created by the same ancient people who had made his ring.

Valentine Grey later let it be known that he had married Jane, but the Church never recognised their open-air marriage in strange white flowing robes, because in law, Valentine was still married, as a Christian, to Anne. All the same, Jane bore her much older 'husband' seven children, and no one knows when Valentine Grey died.

Everyone who knew Valentine and his wife were astonished at their blunt truthfulness, for they never told a lie, and the couple were apparently what we would now term soul-mates, and talked of knowing each other in a bygone golden age. I think that those so-called Bronze Age gold rings were possibly the legendary 'Rings of Truth' said to have been worn by the mystical 'priests' of the ancient Britons. Similar Bronze Age rings have been found on Camp Hill, Woolton Hill and Bidston Hill. Can you imagine how short the career would be of any politician who was forced to wear a Ring of Truth?

~

Another ring that seemed to exhibit a strange power was found on the tracks of Capenhurst Railway Station, Cheshire, one afternoon in 1998. Twelve-year-old Stuart spotted the diamond ring glinting among the gravel and pebbles between the sleepers on the electrified track, and foolishly jumped down off the platform to retrieve it. Had he stumbled, or put a foot wrong, he would surely have been electrocuted, but he was lucky that day. When he had picked up the ring he climbed back on to the platform, then took a close look at the piece of jewellery. It was a silver ring with a purple multi-faceted stone of some sort, and he decided to give it to his mother Louise, who lived in nearby Whitbyheath. Louise had something of a reputation for being psychic, and she had a bad feeling about the ring right from the outset, and told him to throw it away. Stuart, however, had no intention of throwing his treasure away and instead he sold it to a neighbour named Jason for ten pounds.

Jason was delighted with the ring and gave it to his girlfriend in Liverpool, twenty-seven-year-old Kathy, who lived in Aigburth. Kathy showed the ring to her mother, who knew a little about jewellery, and she told her daughter the stone looked as if it was an amethyst. The finger size of the ring was M, and Kathy wore the amethyst on the third finger of her right hand. Three days later, at around 9.30pm, she happened to glance at the ring, and noticed something that initially intrigued her – then terrified her.

There was a small white oval shape in the amethyst. When Kathy brought it closer to her eyes, she saw that the light-coloured shape was in fact a face, just over half a centimetre in length, and she recognised it as that of her friend, Alison. As Kathy scrutinised Alison's face she noticed it seemed to be screaming, but then quick as a flash, the face faded away into nothingness.

Kathy took off the ring and feeling very jittery placed it on the mantelpiece, and took a few steps backwards away from it. She told her mother and brother what had just happened, and her mum, Carol, said it must have been a trick of the light. Kathy's brother Todd picked the ring up, and squinted at the stone, claiming he could see a jumble of shapes in it, but his mother snapped at him, "Leave the thing alone, will you? It's not yours to play with."

Jason arrived the next day and asked Kathy why she wasn't wearing the ring. She told him what had happened, and he said she'd probably just been overtired and seeing things. He pestered her to wear the ring again, and she reluctantly slid it back on her finger. Later that day, bad news arrived at Kathy's Aigburth home in the form of a telephone call from her sister Sarah. Alison's mother had collapsed and died from a heart attack as they were out shopping in the city centre. When the paramedics had arrived and told Alison her mother was dead after several unsuccessful resuscitation attempts, she had screamed and needed sedation.

Kathy went cold as she recalled Alison's silent screaming face in the amethyst, and she took off the ring and threw it in the bin outside. Jason was furious, taking her actions as a rejection, and went to retrieve it. Later that day he had a blazing row with Kathy and they split up for good. Perhaps the previous wearer of that ring had disposed of it on the railway track at Capenhurst because he or she had glimpsed some tragic warning in its stone? If a silver ring of unknown origin and bearing an amethyst comes your way, do be mindful of this story.

SCENT OF FEAR

The following strange incident happened at Halloween 2008, when twenty-two-year-old Jenny visited a lock-up on Roscoe Street, a stone's throw from St Luke's Church, to buy some vintage 1960s stock from her friend Kate. The stock consisted of genuine clothes from the 1960s, such as mini skirts, Pringle sweaters and so on, as well as girls' magazines such as *Honey* and *Petticoat*, and also sealed bottles of perfume from yesteryear such as 'Evening in Paris', and a very rare unopened bottle of perfume from 1966 called 'Detchema'.

Having bought the stock, Jenny took it to her flat on Huskisson Street, where she began sorting it out. Her intention was to then sell these articles to buyers across Liverpool and Manchester who specialised in vintage items. For some reason, Jenny felt drawn to the unopened bottle of Detchema, and she decided to keep the bottle for herself, even though she had no great hopes of the perfume still retaining its original scent. She opened the bottle, sniffed its neck, half expecting the perfume to be sour, considering it was from 1966, and yet a beautiful fragrance, a mixture of peach, carnation, hyacinth and lily of the valley, greeted her nostrils, and she dabbed the scent under each ear.

Being Halloween, Jenny was visited by her friend Claudia, who loved all of the customs associated with Duck-Apple Night. Using cotton thread, Claudia hung up onions, apples, and bars of soap in a doorframe, then she blindfolded Jenny, tied her hands behind her back, and watched her trying to seize the dangling apples with her mouth. She accidentally bit into a bar of soap, and Claudia doubled up with glee as she spat out bits of Palmolive, grimacing from the taste. The atmosphere suddenly changed during this tomfoolery, when Claudia suddenly let out a scream, and ran out of the flat, leaving Jenny still blindfolded with her hands tied behind her back. She initially thought it was all part of the fun and that Claudia was just messing about – getting into the Halloween spirit – but then something terrifying took place. A strong pair of rough masculine hands grabbed her by the shoulders and she winced as she felt a man's stubbly chin rubbing against her neck.

"Hey! Who's that?" Jenny asked, hoping it was all part of the joke. The stranger took deep breaths as he smelt her neck and nuzzled his nose against her earlobe. He then tried to unbutton her top, and she suddenly realised this was no joke. She let out a scream, and tried to run, but being blindfolded, she ran straight into the wall and hit her head. She collapsed unconscious, and the next thing she knew, she was lying in an armchair surrounded by several friends, including Claudia. As she came round, Claudia told a dazed Jenny that she had been startled by the face of a tall man, of Mediterranean appearance, looking out of the wall as Jenny was trying to bite the suspended apples. He then walked out of the wall and grinned menacingly at them both. He wore a brown suede jacket and his irises were almost black under a pair of bushy eyebrows that met in the middle.

Jenny stayed with Claudia for a week before returning to her own flat in Huskisson Street.

Things settled back down again and everything was okay again for almost two months. Then, just before New Years Eve, Jenny again put on the vintage perfume Detchema before leaving her flat, bound for the Belvedere Pub on Sugnall Street. Every step of the way through the misty December streets, she was trailed by a tall dark stranger with long hair. Every fibre of her body was only too well aware of his presence, but at first she could not be sure that he was deliberately following her. Nevertheless she quickened her pace. As she turned the corner into Falkner Street, she could no longer bear the tension and broke into a run. Her worst fears were immediately confirmed when the man responded by sprinting after her. The entire street echoed with her desperate screams as she turned to see how close he was. Too close, but at that moment he vanished before her eyes, but just before he did so, Jenny caught sight of his face. It was contorted with hatred.

A passing student actually witnessed the eerie disappearance of Jenny's stalker, and described him as wearing tight-fitting narrow jeans, ankle-length boots, and a brown suede jacket – exactly matching the description given by Claudia. Going over the events of those two terrible nights, Jenny slowly made the connection between the incidents. Of course! Both times she had been wearing that vintage perfume Detchema and she hasn't used it ever since.

THE CASE OF THE OLD SWAN VAMPIRE

As astonishing as it sounds, Liverpool has quite a history of those mysterious winged creatures of the night – vampires. At the junction of the city's Rupert Lane, Breck Road, Heyworth Street and Everton Road, there lies the skeleton of a man who bit his wife, drank her blood, and, until he had a wooden stake thrust through his body, and was re-interred face down, allegedly rose regularly from his crossroads grave after dark, to terrorise his victims. Thankfully that was all back in 1680, but I have in my files dozens of such reported incidents, stretching right up to the present day.

In the summer of 1866, a gory, shocking murder took place in Liverpool at 14 Wood Grove, which now exists only as a weed-carpeted cul-de-sac off Edge Lane, beside a derelict garage. Yet it was here, in May 1866, that one John Thomas Moss, an outspoken twenty-seven-year-old denouncer of the Christian religion, stayed with his beautiful twenty-five-year-old cousin, Mrs 'Nan' Train, a woman who felt abandoned by her husband Thomas Train, a ship's purser. Moss was rumoured to be a vampire, and people claimed that they had seen his eyes 'light up' like burning coals at the mere mention of Jesus Christ. Despite this, women found themselves unaccountably attracted to him and some even offered to walk out of stable marriages, just so they could wait on him.

For many years Moss lived in Sydney, Australia, as a

cigar manufacturer, but then something must have happened to him, because the John Moss who returned to Liverpool in the early 1860s was not the same happy young fellow who had gone to seek his fortune and a new life in Australia. Very strange stories began to circulate about a suicide attempt at the Albert Dock, and how Moss's lifeless body, dredged from the salty mud at night by some watchmen, was apparently revived by moonlight – one of the many uncanny biological capabilities of a vampire.

Mrs Train had lived under the same roof as Moss for a few years as a lodger, before he was to horrifically murder her. In the Spring of 1866 she and her cousin moved from Elm Vale in Bootle, to Wood Grove, in Liverpool's Old Swan district, and even Mrs Train's husband did not seem to mind Moss's constant presence in their household. It appears that when the cousins were children, they vowed never to separate and, pricking palms and mixing their blood, they ritually sealed their promise.

The only witness to the ghastly murder was twenty-year-old Margaret Golding, Mrs Train's loyal maidservant. She had bravely stayed with her mistress as an enraged Moss had pursued her around the Old Swan residence wielding a hatchet. Mr Train, as usual, was away at sea when these events took place, and Mrs Train was slaughtered because she refused to give Moss a ring, and, more importantly, would not desert her husband and marry him. He ranted on about Hell and the Almighty, loudly rejecting both, and the maid Golding trembled in a corner as his eyes began to glow "as if on fire".

In the frenzied attack, Moss brought the hatchet down on his cousin's head repeatedly, taking off her nose as the blade embedded itself deep in her skull. During one of the ferocious hatchet blows, Mrs Train's eyeball flew out its socket. The maid was so traumatised she was unable to scream, and she found herself running down the stairs, almost in slow motion, as terror got the better of her legs. Behind her, she heard what she would later describe as the sound of a butcher's cleaver hitting bone. When the neighbours and police stormed the house, they found Moss lying in an immense pool of blood on the kitchen floor. He had slit his own throat, and according to the coroner, he had known exactly which arteries to cut in his neck to affect an instantaneous death.

Rumours of vampirism, the stigma of suicide (deemed unholy in those times), and the brutal murder, led to John thomas Moss's body being buried in unconsecrated ground between St Anne's Church, Stanley, and the cattle market. The body was staked, they say, with wood cut from the oldest tree in Liverpool – the Allerton Oak, in Calderstones – which still stands to this day, estimated to be aged over a thousand years old. However, despite these precautions, as you may have guessed, that was not the end of Moss.

Moss's caped form was seen over many evenings in June 1866, lurking in St Mary's Cemetery, Kirkdale, the resting place of his beloved murder victim Mrs Train. A teenaged courting couple, kissing beneath a willow tree in the cemetery, were attacked by the cloaked fiend, but they both managed to make their escape and raised the alarm at a nearby inn. A small posse turned out to hunt down the ghoul, who was seen jumping straight over a five-foot wall at the cemetery, his cloak billowing out behind him.

He also stalked the young maid Margaret Golding in December of that year. The maid had been having terrible vivid blood-spattered nightmares in which she relived the horrors of seeing her mistress being hacked to death. One night she awoke in the early hours in a bedroom at a friend's house in Liverpool's Aigburth district, and felt a strong urge to go to her window. Through a glacial fog, she could see a pale-faced man in black, wearing an opera cloak, but no hat on such an inclement night, standing on the pavement, staring fixedly up at her window. Margaret's heart almost stopped when the man's eyes started to pulsate with a glowing reddish orange tint. Oh, no! Not again, she thought as she recognised John Thomas Moss. As the girl turned and ran out of the room, she heard the window rattling violently behind her, as if someone was trying to prise it open from the outside, but she was too afraid to check, and she awakened the entire household with her screams.

Understandably, Margaret's friend believed the poor girl had suffered nothing more than a particularly lucid nightmare, caused no doubt by the traumatic memories of her employer's horrific murder, but over the next three fog-bound nights, the evil-looking shade of John Thomas Moss was seen by other members of the household, looking in through a basement window of the house, and, according to a neighbour, the cloaked stalker had even been seen on the roof of the Georgian dwelling, apparently trying to break open the skylight window. In the end, a local Catholic priest blessed the house, sprinkled Holy water over the threshold, and gave Margaret a Bible and a Rosary to keep on her bedside table at all times. That seemed to do the trick, and Moss relinquished his sinister pursuit of the former maid.

The Reverend Thomas Gardner, incumbent of St Anne's Church, Stanley, which overlooked the site where Moss had been buried, staked and face down in an unmarked grave on wasteland, warned his congregation in a chilling sermon, about the dangers of succumbing to the dark powers of evil as Moss had. He talked of lost souls wandering the darkest reaches of the earth after death, of demonic persecution and possession, and that other nerve-jangling topic that was doing the rounds in his parish – vampirism.

People living within a mile of the site where Moss lay in his unchristian grave took to taking crosses with them to their beds and hanging garlic from their bedposts, and for many months the churches of the district were guaranteed to be packed every Sunday, as parishioners sought divine protection from the self-resurrected Moss.

Eventually the vampire mania subsided, but even today, there are occasional sightings of a solid, carnate ghost in a cloak, who has been seen in the area of Edge Lane, close to the street where Moss butchered his cousin and then took his own life.

THE VICIOUS CIRCLE

Out in the respectable suburbs of Calderstones, Childwall and Woolton, arcane dark goings-on frequently lurk behind the carefully manicured facades of respectability. Believe it or not, in tree-lined avenues you will find covens of real-life witches, ancient cults of hereditary membership, and secret societies rooted in pre-Christian religions. The same is true of the respectable areas of Wirral, where many bizarre and shocking rituals are enacted behind the lace curtains of suburbia from Hoylake to Neston, and many a respected white collar worker by day has donned grass-green robes, or stripped naked at night to take part in an esoteric rite beneath a full moon on Bidston Hill, or thanked the King of the Wood in Delamere Forest. Some secret societies, though, are rather less sedate in this corner of England, and The Vicious Circle is a case in point.

In the obscure lore of this land I am well versed, and know that February 13th is known as Hatred Day (also called the Day of Blood), when revenge can traditionally be exacted to right old wrongs. On 13 February 1542, Catherine Howard, fifth wife of Henry VIII, was beheaded for high treason. On 13 February 1692, the Government instigated the infamous Glencoe Massacre, and on that same date in 1945, the RAF began the firebombing of Dresden, a town crammed with war refugees, killing 130,000 civilians in a tactic dubbed 'terror bombing', designed to break the German will to fight on. The list goes on ...

In 1968, a rowdy family moved into a house in a tranquil community situated between Hunt's Cross and Woolton Golf Course, shattering the peace and quiet which they valued so highly. The youngest member of this troublesome bunch was an eighteen-year-old skinhead named Ged, whose prize possession was an air rifle. No cat in the neighbourhood was safe and many sustained injuries because of this weapon.

One day, Ged shot the head clean off a pigeon perched on his back-garden fence, and its headless body fluttered blindly into the next door neighbour's bed-sheets hanging out to dry on the washing line in her back-garden, leaving a trail of bloody smears all over them. The neighbour, seventy-year-old Rosemary, warned Ged that he would pay for the barbaric act as he smirked at her before retreating back into his house. To add insult to injury, Ged also threw two eggs over the garden fence later that day, hitting Rosemary's elderly friend Pru and splattering her with egg yolk. The women were incensed that they no longer felt safe in their own gardens and complained to Ged's parents, but they were part of the problem and just swore at the old women, saying their son was "just messing around". Ged and his equally warped older brother John then started a campaign of terror against the two old women, taunting them in the street and calling them, for reasons known best to themselves, "the little piggies".

On the evening of Tuesday, 13 February of that year, as Ged was walking to a friend's house down a secluded lane, a figure stepped out from behind a tree. It was female in shape, though it was indistinct, and wore a

132

quilted, hooded, navy-blue anorak and wielded a cricket bat. The face was obscured by a bizarre plastic cartoon pig mask. Ged stood rooted to the spot, and the stranger started belting him with the bat, so he turned to run, whereupon another female figure, also hooded, and wearing the same type of mask, clobbered Ged with a hockey stick, cutting his ear and badly bruising his neck and jaw. In a state of terror, the thug dived straight through a prickly hedge screaming in agony.

That same morning, someone had carefully opened the delivered milk bottles on Ged's doorstep to pour red paint in them and presumably the same mischief-maker had plugged both keyholes of the skinhead's front and back doors with cement the night before, ruining the locks. The old woman next door was confronted by Ged's heavily tattooed father, but Rosemary just shook her head and innocently replied that such reprisals against bad people always took place on February 13th, with it being Hatred Day. Ged's cowardly dad threatened that if there were any more incidents he'd put in Rosemary's windows and string her cat up. Then, after giving her the V-sign, he stormed back to his house, muttering a string of obscenities under his breath.

A week later, when the family were out, someone evidently broke into their home and nailed a stinking, rotten fish to the underside of their dining table. A razor blade was left embedded in a bar of bath soap, and maggots were strewn about the carpets and furniture in the living room. The family returned home late to find a bizarre calling card in the hallway, which read: 'The Vicious Circle called today'. In a rage, Ged's father banged on next door's door to have it out with Rosemary, but he got the shock of his life when twenty people, all wearing weird masks, swarmed out of the house and formed a tight circle round him. All of these strangers were armed with hatchets and pick-axe handles, though they did not threaten him with them. Not a word was spoken, nor needed to be, by the menacing masked strangers, but it finally dawned on Ged's father exactly who the Vicious Circle were, and, in an uncharacteristic admission of defeat and submission, he and his family packed up and left the area that night.

~

A Mrs Coyne wrote to me about the Vicious Circle vigilantes in 2002. From 1968 to 1975, Mrs Coyne lived in Halewood, and during the summer of 1971, there were a number of burglaries in her neighbourhood. Residents had their suspicions regarding the identity of the housebreakers, but were too afraid to go to the police for fear of reprisals. One night in the local pub, Mrs Coyne noticed a tall man of about fifty-something walking into the parlour and she recalled that he had the air of an ex-military man about him. He ordered a short, then looked around, surveying the clientele. His eyes settled on a group of men playing darts and after knocking back his drink in one gulp, he went over to them and disrupted their game by snatching the set of darts that had just been thrown at the board before they could retrieve them. Turning to two of the players, who were the men suspected of being the housebreakers, the stranger issued a threat: "If you continue what you're doing, you'll end up in hospital."

"What're you talking about, mate?" asked one of the darts players, a young man of about twenty. He was much smaller than the stranger, but wasn't frightened of confronting him in a cocky manner. The outsider just smiled, put his glass down on the bar and then, still clutching the confiscated darts, left, deliberately knocking the young man out of the way as he made for the door. Something about his manner stopped any of the men from retaliating.

Nobody thought much further about this incident until three days later, when two local houses were burgled. During one of these burglaries, a child's brand new bike, given to him as a birthday present, was stolen. On the following morning, at 6am, a milkman doing his rounds came upon a bizarre sight. The two burglars responsible for the series of break-ins were found unconscious, bound to a lamppost standard with black eyes and cuts to their faces.

The word soon went around that the Vicious Circle were responsible for giving the criminals a good hiding, and one of the crooks himself admitted that he had received a menacing phone call in the dead of night, warning him that he was being watched by the secret vigilante organisation, on the eve of his beating. The burglars left the Halewood area shortly after they were beaten up (allegedly by seven people wearing masks) and then left on humiliating display for all the neighbourhood to see.

I have received many more similar accounts of secret vigilante groups, but the Vicious Circle seems to have disbanded around the mid-1970s.

THE WATCHER

One January afternoon in 1965, two girls, both aged nineteen, met up in Bold Street's El Kabala coffee bar. Donna worked at the Saxone shoe shop in Church Street, and Maureen at the Maypole supermarket in nearby Lord Street, but today both girls had a day off, and for once, they were both free as a bird, each having chucked their pitiful boyfriends for various reasons.

Donna soon confided that she had both good news and bad news, and as usual dragged it out until Maureen swore in frustration and told her to get to the point or shut up. Donna's favourite uncle had died, and he had left her five hundred pounds, which, in 1965, was worth ten times more than that sum is worth today.

"Oh my god! What're you going to do with it, Don?" Maureen asked, sipping a coffee.

"Well, I was thinking of moving out of ours and renting a flat," Donna replied.

She even knew which flat she wanted; it was a first floor one in an old semi on Woolton Road, near Childwall. The rent was very reasonable, just five pounds a week.

At this point, Bernie, a thirty-seven-year-old man, reached over from the neighbouring table and touched Donna's arm, startling her. Bernie had used to live near Donna in Kensington, and was something of a stalker who would follow her from school, even though she had been only fourteen and he was thirty-two at the time.

"Hey there, glamour puss, I live up in Woolton Road," he informed Donna, who pretended she hadn't heard him.

"Let's go, Mo," she said to Maureen and they both left the coffee bar with their drinks half finished.

Donna went ahead and moved into the flat, and being nervous because Bernie might still be hanging around, she asked Maureen to stay with her most nights. A fortnight later, the girls had just finished watching the television at around 9.30pm, when Maureen went into the kitchen. "Where's that Mantuna tea packet, Donna?" she asked, searching the cupboard. "It was here this morning."

"In the tea caddy! By the window!"

Maureen went to get the caddy, which was where Donna said it was, but as she glanced out the window, she noticed something eerie; a square of dim yellow light in the distance – someone's window – but near enough for Maureen to make out the figure of a man who seemed to be watching her.

"When are you getting nets for these windows Donna?" she called out. She then turned the kitchen light off and urged Donna to come into the kitchen. She pointed out the weird watcher, but Donna said, "How d'you know he's watching us? You must have good eyesight. Switch the light back on."

Maureen refused, but Donna insisted and waved at the silhouette in the distance. "See, he can't even see us, he's that far away." But after a short delay of a few seconds the figure slowly waved back and then kept up his vigil for the rest of that night. The girls tried to put a net curtain up in the kitchen, but the hooks kept falling out of the plaster. A handyman then fitted a blind, but it jammed and couldn't be pulled down. Every night, like clockwork at around 9pm, the watcher would appear at his window. Donna gave him the V sign out of anger. Then, fearing it might encourage him to pay a visit, she waved instead, but this time he did not wave back.

Donna's brother came to visit and had the nosy parker pointed out to him. He didn't like the idea one bit of some weirdo ogling his sister every night, so he set off into the Woolton night to confront him. Some time later he returned to the flat baffled, because he had not been able to locate the house.

A week later, Donna mislaid her purse. She knew that it was somewhere in the house, but she searched high and low for it without success. Then the telephone rang and a gruff-voiced caller, who didn't identify himself, told her – quite correctly as it turned out – that the purse was behind the letter-rack on the mantelpiece. Sure enough, there it was. Though relieved to have found it, Donna was unnerved by the idea that a stranger should have known where it was. Had he been in the flat? Maybe he had even hidden it. Instinctively she glanced out of the kitchen window; there was the creepy watcher, at his post as usual, waving to her from his window about four hundred yards away. She immediately telephoned Maureen, even though it was 11pm, to tell her what had happened.

"I'm sorry, I can't come over tonight, Donna," Maureen told her frightened friend. "Our little Billy's not well and I'm looking after him on me own … me mam and dad have gone out."

Donna really wanted Maureen's company that night, but she understood that she couldn't leave Billy. She told Maureen that she was thinking of going back to stay in her parent's house for the night.

"Nah, don't be going out at this hour, Donna," Maureen advised. "Just stay in and watch the telly; I'm watching *On the Braden Beat*. It's good. Just lock the doors, Donna. You'll be alright, and phone me if you get a bit scared, okay?"

"Yeah, okay, Mo," said Donna uncertainly, and she then voiced a concern that had been playing on her mind for some time about the weird stalker Malcolm, who they'd bumped into in the Bold Street coffee bar. Hadn't he said he lived up on Woolton Road – where Donna now lived, but Maureen dismissed the idea.

"Nah, it won't be him, Donna, he's just away with the mixer, and how would he know your phone number anyway? It'll just be some idiot having a laugh. I'd just phone the police if he starts that lark."

Nervously, Donna settled down to watch the television. She had also put the radio on in the kitchen, as well as every light in the flat. It lessened her anxiety somehow, and created the impression that she was not alone in the place.

Around midnight, as the television networks closed down, Donna went into the kitchen and noticed a bottle of QC Wine she had bought the other day for her and Maureen to share the next time she came round. She opened the bottle and took it into the living room, where she started reading her horoscope in the newspaper and tried to relax. She polished off the entire bottle of wine in forty minutes, and it filled her with Dutch courage. She staggered tipsily into the kitchen and waved at the uncanny shadowy figure of the watcher at his window in the depth of the nightscape. He showed no reaction, so, behaving in a way she would never have done if she were sober, Donna lifted up her polo-neck to show her bra. She then beckoned the creepy observer with both hands, laughed and went to lie on her sofa, because she felt light-headed.

An hour later she got up and went to the toilet, but as she passed the living room window, she automatically looked out and saw something odd: for once, the peeping Tom was not at his window. Coming back from the toilet, she went into the kitchen to make herself a cup of coffee in an effort to sober up. As she filled the kettle, she looked out of the window, and was shocked to see a man's face, up close, looking in on her. He wasn't on a ladder – but floating outside in the night air, and he grinned with amusement as Donna dropped the kettle and then screamed.

"Donna!" the levitating man shouted in that all too familiar gruff voice that had been heard on the telephone. Donna was so terrified, she ran out of the flat leaving the tap running and the plug in the plughole. By the time she came back in the morning, the kitchen was flooded and the floor ruined. She quickly collected together her belongings and abandoned the flat; her short experiment in independent living brought to an abrupt end.

The ghost of the 'watcher' is still being seen in the Woolton Road area, according to ongoing reports I have received at Radio Merseyside, so do keep your curtains drawn after dark if you live in that area, because someone may be watching you ...

PUPPET POSSESSION

Between villain and priest, between good and evil, there is but a short spectrum of personality shades that vary by degrees. Beyond the zebra crossing and chequerboard, few things in life are black and white, and the same goes for people's personas – to some degree, there is a cocktail mixture of saint and devil in most individuals, and this was the case with thirty-five-year-old John Brown and sixty-nine-year-old Billy Hepton. Both had bad reputations, both were troublesome vagrants, heavy drinkers (when money was available) and occasional shoplifters, but deep down, they had hearts of gold.

On a sunny golden but Arctic morning in February 1977, John and Billy stood in front of a premises at 108-112 Bold Street. John, with an old Bic pen in one hand and a card beer-mat (with one side peeled off) in the other, was taking dictated notes from Billy, as he surveyed the well-stocked windows of the House of Holland store. "A set of six dining chairs and mahogany table, and erm, a pouffe …" Billy was saying.

"How do you spell pouffe?" asked John.

"Don't know," Billy replied, "just put puff. We'll also be needing an electric kettle, a stainless steel five-piece tea set, and erm, an upright vacuum cleaner."

"What else then?" John asked, after painstakingly jotting the items down.

Billy pressed his purple black-pored nose to the

window pane. "That quilt there ... and write king-size next to it."

"Two ... king-size ... quilts. We'll be needing two beds as well." John muttered, still writing everything down, but then his pen ran dry with the cold.

Billy shook his head, "Nah just the one quilt, you get more heat sleeping together. We'll get the bed sorted soon."

"I'm not sleeping with you, Billy. I'm not one of *them*," was stunned John's reply.

Billy became annoyed, "Hey, don't flatter yourself, mate! I'm no Nancy boy neither but it'd be warmer ... that's all I'm saying. Oh forget it, Mr Problem!"

They walked up Bold Street, both knowing full well they would never get the money together to buy furniture and things for their place – a condemned old house in Toxteth. The two tramps had met on the Pier Head Landing Stage one day three years back, both intending to commit suicide because of their chronic drink problems, but each talking the other one out of the act. At the edge of letting go of this world, the two men had bonded but had remained together in the brotherhood of the bottle.

On that bleak February day, John and Billy got 'home' at 11.30am to find a JCB and a gang of men knocking their place down, and they both dissolved into tears. A gang of children, amused at seeing two grown men crying, first started throwing water-filled balloons at them, but then had a sudden change of heart. The kids went and raided the larders of their homes and brought back some packets of Bovril crisps, some Nice biscuits and even some cigarettes – but no matches, and gave them to the two now homeless men.

One little girl gave a soaked John her father's sheepskin coat – unbeknown to her father, who was fortunately at work. There happened to be a ten-pound note in the pocket of that sheepskin coat, and when Billy caught John trying to hide it, he slapped his face, knocking his glass eye out. Luckily it didn't crack upon hitting the pavement, but rolled along Windsor Street, where it was stopped under the sole of a policeman's boot. The PC picked up the glass eye, and handed it back to John – then, without an ounce of sympathy in his soul, moved John and Billy on. Billy apologised to his friend for striking him, and the two vagrants quickly made up their quarrel.

Bottles of cider and whisky were purchased, and, wandering through icy rain and hail as far as Aigburth, the inebriated duo stumbled across a derelict Edwardian house, within a stone's throw of Sefton Park, which could only be accessed via a broken backyard door in an alleyway. This became their new home, in "a more up-market area", according to Billy. John had reservations about the detached house, which had been abandoned in that dark era of municipal neglect and left forgotten among the numerous sycamore saplings which had sprung up around it, obscuring it from view.

John's misgivings about the empty dwelling arose when he noticed the 'tramp marks' chalked near the back door of the house. Many seasoned career vagrants leave signs, carved and chalked near houses where they have stopped to beg; signs which mean nothing to the uninitiated, but are there to warn and inform others of their mendicant class. A circle with a spot in the centre, a triangle, a square or a letter T tipped to the right, are all warning signs that tramps use across the world to show

143

their colleagues what type of people live in the vicinity. A square denotes 'bad people', the T symbol tilted at 45 degrees means 'no good', and a triangle means 'too many tramps have been here already' – but chalked on the back wall of the dilapidated house was the sign of the circle enclosing a central dot, which means 'very bad – avoid at all costs'. But as there was no living soul in the old house, Billy Hepton decided to disregard the warning symbol, even though it looked freshly chalked.

By the following day John and Billy were close to pennilessness once again. Billy stole two bottles of gold top milk from an elderly woman's doorstep and when the milk went off and became semi-solid, Billy hung his sock up by a nail on the parlour wall and poured the sour milk into the sock to strain it. Eventually it would curdle and they would have cheese, he claimed. Billy had eaten wood pigeons from the park in tougher times. "But they're all bones," he told a disgusted John.

Before his descent into the abyss of alcoholism and street-begging, John had been an electrician, so it was straightforward enough for him – even with the shaking hand of the DT's – to establish an electricity supply to the house, via an outside heavy voltage cable, to a fuse-box in the cellar. John, however, knew his limitations and decided, rather wisely, not to reconnect the gas supply to the rundown house.

Until an electric fire could be cadged or stolen, the tramps had to make do with the good old-fashioned open fire, and newspapers scavenged from dustbins and dry twigs gathered from Sefton Park provided quite an efficient fuel. Night came. Billy was quite proud of two thick fallen branches of ash he'd spotted in the park, and after cutting them to size with a rust-coated saw found in the cellar, he placed his logs, and a bunch of thin hazel twigs, found by John, in the grate. Lying on his coat, which was rolled out on the bare floorboards, Billy sat smoking a filtered cigarette, watching the flames lick around the logs. "Who needs radiators, gas and electricity when we've got the glowing cheerfulness of living flames like this, eh?" he sighed, smugly. He looked around the vast room, at the crimson and orange lights playing across the ceiling, projected by the growing spears of fire from the grate. The heat proved almost feverish in that indoor hearthrug summer, as the spreading crystals of a February frost turned the outside world silvery-white under the winter moon. John, seated on his treasured sheepskin, basked in the steady glow of the fire, lost in luxurious meditation, that was until his thoughts turned to where their next meal, and more importantly, their next drink, were coming from. Billy's home-made cheese from the sock did not sound appetising, nor did his roasted Sefton Park wood pigeons. John decided instead to resort to prayer, believing he had had nothing but bad luck after ceasing all communication with his god many years ago.

"God ... if you exist," he began haltingly, with clenched eyelids, "... and if you don't, well I suppose it doesn't matter, because I'm only talking to myself ... but, if you do, send us money please ... we really do need some money ... it's urgent."

John couldn't even remember the words of the Lord's Prayer, and was only too well aware that his attempts at praying were abyssmal.

Billy smiled sarcastically as he heard his friend's 'prayer' and he came out with a spiritual request of his own, but he pitched it at God's ancient enemy: "And if

you exist, Mr Devil, please change our luck, thank you!"
Adding to the floorboards, "But if I'm talking to myself,
then just ignore me.'

The tramps then lay down under their coats, with
newspaper bundles for pillows. Within minutes, John
was snoring, and Billy too was just dozing off when he
thought he heard singing upstairs. He listened, and as the
singing stopped, the sound of footsteps could be heard.
Someone was creaking his way down the stairs. Billy
scarcely dared breathe, and then he heard the footsteps
stop right outside the parlour. The doorknob squeaked as
it slowly turned. The door inched open and in came a
strangely dressed man. His dark hair was slicked back
and pressed close against his domed head. He wore a
monocle, and his attire looked a little militaristic
comprising a black shirt and black trousers tucked into
black leather boots. He also wore an armband which
featured a reversed Z-shaped lightning strike.

Billy recalled the uniform from his younger years; the
stranger was dressed as a 'blackshirt' – a British member
of Oswald Mosley's Nazi-styled British Union of Fascists
party – but surely they had only been a product of the
1930s Depression and had been disbanded years ago?

"John!" Billy cried, and instantly the man in black
vanished.

John had been in the middle of a beautiful dream
about the early courting days with his wife Gracie, whom
he hadn't seen in years, and Billy's cry had awakened
him from that blissful refuge from reality. He was so
angry. "What?" he shouted.

"This place is haunted," Billy replied, his eyes
transfixed on the door, which was still open.

John groaned as he sat up and got to his feet. "All that

146

drinking's pickling your mind," he said, seemingly unaware of the irony of what he was saying. "Every bottle you knock back kills over a billion brain cells; a scientist on that telly programme *Horizon* said so," he continued in a pompous voice. Crossing the floor, he closed the door, and returned to his hearthside bed, reassuring Billy that nothing more sinister than a draught had opened the door. John was soon snoring again, and somehow, Billy managed to fall asleep, albeit with his face hidden under his coat.

Billy awoke to piercing screams at 4am, but it was nothing supernatural this time. A cockroach had crawled into John's open mouth as he had lain snoring, and the spat-out bug was scuttling back across the floorboards into the safety of some crevice.

By the following morning, Billy had dismissed the appearance of the ghostly blackshirt as some lucid dream, and he went out to steal the bottles of silver-top milk from the doorstep of a house around the corner, and returned singing merrily. "The morning has gold in its mouth, full of opportunity," he told a bleary-eyed, crumple-faced John, who was still dwelling on the cockroach incident.

Around nine, Billy was to be found mooching about amongst the rubble in the damp draughty attic. On the floor, amid the heterogeneous mess which an army of woodlice had made their home, he came across an old monocle, and immediately recalled the monocle the blackshirt had worn. Still trying to convince himself that the ghost had all been in his mind, he picked up the eyepiece, wiped the thick layer of dust away with a handkerchief, and looked through it. It definitely improved the vision in his weak left eye.

In a corner, under the eaves, Billy then noticed a large brown packing case in the corner. Having eagerly undone the catches and opened it up, he smiled gleefully. Lying stretched out in the case was some sort of bald-headed ventriloquist's dummy, dressed in a tatty tuxedo. Billy lifted it out of the box and ran his fingers over its face. It felt and looked like smoothed plaster that had been painted with flesh-coloured emulsion, which was flaking off in places. Immediately, the possibility of a money-making ventriloquist act on the thoroughfares and street-corners of Liverpool sprang to mind. It would definitely beat his penny whistle performance outside the Lyceum. He didn't know the first thing about ventriloquism, but he confidently believed he could acquire the skill with a little practice. He put his hand inside the doll's back, and suddenly became incredibly well acquainted with the strings and levers which controlled the dummy. They seemed so familiar. It was all quite strange but oddly satisfying.

In the toilet of the ruined Aigburth house, a constipated John sat reading the 'Your Stars' tabloid column of astrologer June Penn, trying to determine whether his luck was about to change, when the shiny-head of the dummy came peeping around the warped lavatory door. Its hinged mouth opened wide, and its eerie dark-rimmed eyes rolled around as Billy rasped, "Peek a boo!" John Brown gave a startled grunt and flung the newspaper at the sinister face, which withdrew from the toilet to the sounds of Billy's loud guffaws.

That day, the vagrants tried to dream up names for the dummy. "Qualtrough", Billy kept saying, but John had his own suggestions: Dilly Dally, Tom Tiddler, Joe Soap, Cheeky Charlie, and so on, but Billy dismissed each

148

suggestion with a shake of his head, as the mouth of the dummy opened and said, "My name is Qualtrough."

John was really impressed with the voice projection. "I didn't know you could throw your voice, Billy."

Neither did I, thought Billy. "My first performance shall be at the Lyceum!" he announced with a bow, picturing the Lyceum Theatre in London, where he had once worked many years ago as a stage-hand. Instead they headed for the top of the steps of the soot-coated Lyceum at the bottom of Bold Street and a crowd soon gathered around the act. John was the straight man, and Qualtrough displayed the combined wit of Oscar Wilde and Woody Allen, coupled with a surreal type of comedy way ahead of its time. The policeman who moved the tramps on saw the cap full of collected money, and said to the dummy, "You're not as stupid as you look!" to which Qualtrough replied, "No, but you are, constable," which delighted the crowd.

Next stop was the Pier Head, where Billy swigged a bottle of purple meths as Qualtrough sang 'Winchester Cathedral'. Even Reppy, the grouchiest tramp in Liverpool, clapped along and conceded that the ventriloquism was "extraordinary" – and then he almost pulled the head off the dummy as he tried to steal it from Billy. There was a scuffle, a punch was thrown by Reppy, missed, and hit a young sailor enjoying his leave. The sailor knocked Reppy's only tooth clean out.

Over sixty pounds was taken that day, and Billy Hepton used some of the proceeds to get a short back and sides and an extra-close shave at a barber's on Leece Street. Then the barber was instructed to slick Billy's new hairstyle back with a generous helping of Brylcreem. As the barber stemmed the tiny nick on Billy's face with styptic chalk, he told the vagrant's mirror image that he looked as if he had been reborn. Billy then bought a pin-striped suit in Oxfam, and instead of buying the usual whisky and lager at the off licence, he purchased menthol cigarettes, a bottle of Chardonnay, and a set of wine glasses from Lewis's. He started to speak with a Noel Coward accent and held long conversations with Qualtrough, which nearly drove John to distraction. Each night, Billy would put Qualtrough to 'bed' in his case, kiss his forehead, cover him with a blanket and sing Hoagy Carmichael's 'Stardust' to the doll.

Enough was enough, and one morning at 3am, John got up in a drunken state, unable to sleep, and quietly removed Qualtrough from its case. Billy was nowhere to be seen; then John heard him upstairs in the toilet. John folded Qualtrough so his little polished black brogues touched the back of that bald plaster head. With teeth-grinding hatred the dummy was placed on the fire and dowsed with meths. There was a loud 'whumph!' as the meths combusted and John drew back with a singed left eyebrow and fringe. Qualtrough's eyes and mouth shot open wide as he shrieked within the enveloping fireball. John staggered backwards, sobered by the shock of what he had done to Billy's beloved 'son'. Suddenly the burning dummy came alive and crawled out of the fireplace, rolled around, trying to extinguish the flames, and frantically patted its wooden hands around the smoking tuxedo. "You stupid bastard!" it screamed at John.

In sheer terror, the tramp grabbed a rusty old poker and brought it down on Qualtrough's head. Plaster fragments and blood flecked with pink matter flew everywhere. John ran out of the room, his legs numb with fear, and collided with Billy, who was walking groggily along the hallway on his way back from the toilet, half asleep. He saw his precious doll aflame, and the vivid red blood oozing from the gaping hole in its head, bubbling and spitting as it hit the hot coals. He tried to go to its aid, but John dragged him out of the house.

"You murderer! You cold-blooded murderer!" Billy screamed in his well-spoken accent.

"It's just a bloomin' doll, Billy!"

"You killed a child! You killed little Qualtrough!" Billy screamed, and he threw a punch at John but missed, and fell on the icy surface of the drive, which was like as cast-iron. Fire spread quickly through the old dilapidated house and Qualtrough's screams could be heard amongst the crackling blaze. Just before the fire engines arrived, Billy seemed to snap out of some hypnotic spell and the Noel Coward accent faded away. He dashed the monocle to the ground and crushed it under his boot.

Billy later confessed to John that he had been utterly possessed by the spirit of the ventriloquist, who had somehow haunted the weird dummy that he had once operated. Billy believed this spirit also manifested itself as the ghost of the blackshirt he had seen in the parlour that night, and the vagrant had also sensed that the unknown fascist had been a murderer with a terrible temper and a twisted, evil mind. The tramps hurried away from the blaze across moonlit Liverpool in search of another old empty house as far away from Aigburth as possible.

GHOSTS THAT TERRIFY

One moonlit night at 1.20am, in the summer of 1983, fifteen-year-old Hannah left her mother's house on Kirkby's Old Rough Lane and, against her mum's wishes, set off for her father's home off Whitefield Drive, a journey of just over a mile, which Hannah usually completed in about ten to fifteen minutes. The girl's parents had separated three years back, and on this balmy summer's morning, Hannah had had something of a tiff with her mother, so she had decided to go and stay with her dad for the night. She stormed off in a sulk, crossed the junction of County Road and Hall Lane, and soon found herself walking down the eerie secluded lane that runs alongside St Chad's graveyard, Old Hall Lane, regretting her impulsiveness. A low sandstone wall, about two-and-a-half feet tall, was to her right, and only this divide separated her from the forest of gravestones.

Hannah hurried down this isolated lane, humming a tune in an effort to stop her mind dwelling on the uncanny graveyard shadows and peculiar quality of the moonlight – a sombre luminosity that could only be described as a type of 'dead' daylight. Straight ahead, creeping towards her, there rolled a very low ground-mist from the far end of the lane, like a blanket unfolding. Hannah slowed down, wary of the ominous thick white night vapour, because there was something quite unnatural about the way it rolled forward without dispersing, almost as if it were liquid – and under intelligent control. Then the mist stopped sliding along the ground, and rose instead into a column that coalesced into the figure of a tall man! Hannah stopped dead, her heart pounding in her ears. The vapour had been transformed into a tall, abnormally thin man, well over six feet in height with a pasty white face and black skull-socket eyes. His stringy grey hair was collar-length and hung from each side of a skull-like head that was balding on top. The menacing apparition wore a black outdated suit from some bygone era, and a white shirt with a collar that stood upright. The man's mouth opened wider and wider, visible to the traumatised teenager as a gaping black hole that kept on enlarging until it reached unnatural proportions, then emitted a loud tormented groan, and started to trot towards Hannah, making a loud clicking sound as it did so, as if he had metal studs on the heels and soles of its long tapering shoes.

In a dreamlike state, Hannah turned round, her legs weakening, and she made a single grunting sound as she tried to scream but found herself hopelessly unable to. She heard the spectre getting closer as its studs hit the pavement with a rhythmic sound that grew in intensity with each determined stride, and the girl summoned up enough energy to suddenly bolt away up Old Hall Lane. The ghost repeatedly issued bloodcurdling screams as Hannah reached Hall Lane, and she was too terrified to slow down enough to look back. She too started to scream at this point, and prayed that someone would hear her, but there wasn't a living soul about at that hour. She finally reached her mother's house and hammered on the front door, but when she glanced to the left, she saw the tall ghost running towards her, about thirty yards

153

away. She started to cry, and her mother, standing in the hallway on the other side of the front door, asked who was calling.

"It's me, mum! Let me in," Hannah sobbed, and slapped her hand repeatedly on the door.

Her mother drew back the bolt and undid the Yale lock. She opened the door, and Hannah lunged forward with such force she almost knocked her over. Her mother guessed she was fleeing from someone, and instinctively slammed the door shut and began to slide the bolt. Footsteps with those distinctive tap tapping studs could be heard outside, coming to a halt in front of the door. Hannah ran panting into the living room and told her mother what had taken place, and her mum was worried that the thing chasing might not have been a ghost, but some deranged pervert. "I'm calling the police," she said, and reached for the telephone, but when the police promptly arrived, they were sceptical about the account Hannah gave them of her strangely-dressed pursuer. All the same, they agreed to patrol the area for a while and keep a lookout for the 'oddball' as they called him.

Hannah and her mother stayed up late, waiting for the summer dawn to chase away the eventful night, but at 3.15am, the tall ghostly man was back. Hannah's mother was the first to spot him peering through the window of the front room, and ran upstairs to take a better look at the weird stalker from the bedroom window with her daughter. From behind the curtains, they saw the terrifying apparition gazing up at them with his black-holed eyes, and a fiendish grin of crooked teeth. Mother and daughter recoiled in terror from the window, and refused to go to bed until the sun was up.

After that eventful night, Hannah and her mother

never again set eyes on the lanky ghoul of Old Hall Lane, but other people have had strange and often frightening experiences in the vicinity of St Chad's cemetery. At the end of Old Hall Lane, near Kirkby Bridge, and in nearby Milbrook Park, the lower half of a man's trousered legs have been seen walking around, always at dusk. There are similar accounts of ghosts with deteriorated images, in which only part of the apparition is visible. A case in point was the disembodied legs of a woman that were seen pacing around the Girobank building in Bootle many years ago. Around the time the Girobank building was being built, a female student was allegedly murdered by a watchman and dumped on the building site one night. The killer covered the body under rubble that was due to be encased in concrete the next morning, but the victim's legs were spotted protruding from the debris, and the corpse was uncovered. Some think the ghostly legs somehow mirrored the victim's legs as they had been seen sticking out from the rubble.

The disconcerting phantom legs that walk Old Hall Lane, Kirkby Row and Milbrook Park have yet to be explained, and a female medium who investigated several sightings of this partially materialised ghost thinks there is some paranormal connection with Kirkby Brook, which runs through the area of the hauntings.

In the 1970s, a practising witch dowsing with a hazel twig detected what she described as a powerful vortex of 'telluric' earth-energy emanating from the length of Kirkby Brook that passes close to Old Hall Lane and St Chad's Cemetery. Perhaps the whirlpool of energy given off by the brook is somehow responsible for the various hauntings in the area, and other paranormal goings-on, such as the well-documented sightings of Little

155

People in St Chad's Churchyard in the 1960s. Long before Norse invaders settled in Kirkby and named it Cherchebi, the land St Chad's church was built upon (by the fifth Earl of Sefton in 1871), there existed an earlier chapel, also dedicated to St Chad, which was constructed in 870 AD, when the Saxon King Ethelred I ruled Wessex and Kent. Before this period, the site on which the Chapel of St Chad was built was already revered by the ancient peoples who had settled in that part of Lancashire, and they may have followed a 'nature religion' similar to the Druids. Another site revered by the locals was a plot of earth now covered by St Mary's Church, Northwood, which, for centuries has been the scene of many reports of the Little People.

~

Many years ago, in 1964, there was a spate of terrifying encounters with what can only be described as a 'ghoul' in the areas of Mossley Hill, Woolton and West Derby. The first report comes from thirteen-year-old Greg, who was homeward bound one rainy evening in November 1964. Greg lived on Limedale Road, off Allerton Road, and had just been playing football on the triangular green of Menlove Gardens until the worsening rain and gathering gloom brought the game to an end. To reach home the boy had to cross busy Menlove Avenue near the roundabout, and take a shortcut down Wyndcote Road. The time was fast approaching 10pm when Greg stopped to tie his shoelace at the corner of Wyndcote Road, and it was there that he saw something which would lodge in his memory for ever more.

A weird-looking individual, with tufts of wild reddish air sprouting from either side of a bulbous bald head, was lurking in the shadows, beyond the rays of the nearby streetlamp. His face was elongated, and contained a cavernous mouth which moved in a peculiar circular motion as he ate, very reminiscent of the way a camel chews. The large broad teeth of the ghastly-looking figure were making a loud cracking and grating sound, and the eyes seemed to have a faint golden glow about them.

Greg skirted around the man, giving him a wide berth, sensing he was evil, and noticed the corpse of a dog lying by the man's feet. A trail of blood ran from the carcass into the gutter in Menlove Avenue; the poor creature had obviously been struck, and most probably killed, by a car.

The ghoul was grasping a severed leg from this dead dog as though it were a piece of cooked chicken. With mounting horror, Greg realised that he was actually biting great chunks out of the dead dog and then eating them – hence the exaggerated chewing motion. As the boy whimpered in fear and felt his legs go weak, the ghoul let out a derisive laugh, and started to walk towards him. Greg tried to run, but his head felt dizzy. He had just made it to the nearest house on Wyndcote Road, intending to hammer on the door-knocker for help, when the ghoul let out a hissing sound, like a car radiator bursting then turned and ran off, still clutching the dog's leg. Greg ran off home, fighting back the tears, for he was an animal lover and had a dog of his own.

Three days later, at the launderette on Allerton Road, Greg's mother Elsie met a former neighbour, a Mrs Lethbridge, and the two of them got talking and about this and that. In the course of the conversation, Mrs Lethbridge mentioned a strange incident which sent a shiver up Elsie's spine.

Her son Sam had been out courting with his girlfriend Barbara near the municipal golf course the previous night. They had been "kissing and carrying on" she said, by Allerton Golf Lodge, when a very peculiar-looking man had passed them in the moonlight, quite unaware that he was being watched. Sam and Barbara saw this man chase a fox across the green, throwing a huge knife at the animal several times until it managed to escape. The stranger then walked towards Sam and Barbara, and from closer quarters they could see that his appearance was quite terrifying. Mrs Lethbridge's description of the man matched Greg's report: the bulbous bald head, the sprouts of wild reddish hair, glowing eyes and peculiar over-sized animal-like jaws and prominent teeth. The uncanny prowler produced a long bladed knife, and tapped it against his hand as he smiled wickedly at Sam and Barbara, and the lovers fled from the golf course and didn't stop running until they reached Barbara's home on Rose Lane.

The same ghoul-like entity was later seen around 11.40pm one foggy night in December of that year in Hayman's Green, West Derby, near to the grounds of a bowling club. On that occasion, it was seen by a policeman, and when he was challenged, he ran off into Mill Lane and seemed to vanish before he could get close to him.

What surely has to be the same supernatural being was seen just before Christmas that year, prowling Springwood Cemetery in Allerton. The descriptions given by three witnesses who had just left the cemetery to pay their respects to lost loved ones all matched, but despite an immediate search of the grounds by police, the sinister figure was nowhere to be seen, but many years later, one of the policemen involved in the search for the ghoul told me how he felt as if he and his colleagues were being closely watched that late afternoon in 1960, as they scoured the place of the dead for clues. "I could literally feel that thing's eyes boring into the back of my head, and I was only too glad to leave the cemetery," says the policeman, now in his seventies.

In the lore of the supernatural, a ghoul is a demonic being that feeds on the flesh of humans and animals, but especially children and travellers. They typically haunt graveyards, ruins and similarly secluded places. In the past, ghouls have been said to steal bodies from graves for nourishment, and one of these beings is said to prowl Allerton Tower after dark, just a short distance from the spot where Sam and Barbara saw their ghoul in 1960. The name 'ghoul' is derived from the Arabic name for the demon – ghula – and the creature seems to be reported in almost every religion and culture. The ghoul that is alleged to roam Allerton is said to spend long periods of rest in a secret grave, only awakening every few years to feast on the living and the dead. I first heard of this spine-chilling creature when I was a child, but I am told it is a very old local legend that dates back to the 1930s at least.

THE STRANGE VISITANTS OF DR WALLACE

On the evening of Wednesday, 10 February 1886, one of the most highly respected physicians in Lancashire, Dr John Wallace, was checking on the symptoms of a rare condition in a medical textbook. Beyond the panes of the first-floor window of his study, at Number 1 Gambier Terrace, a hair-thin smiling crescent moon hung over St James's Mount, where the Anglican Cathedral would one day stand. Deserted Hope Street below was dusted with a sparse February snow that glittered in the lamplight. Dr Wallace lit a cigar, and was about to partake of a glass of fine port, when he caught sight of something in the sky outside the window. He gently moved the curtain aside to afford a better view of a pale semi-transparent female figure in a flowing gauze-like shroud, as she floated down towards the window from rooftop level. Wallace backed away from the drapes and edged towards his writing bureau, transfixed by the unearthly visitor, who glided into the room as if the window had no substance.

Dr Wallace recognised the ghost – if indeed that was what it was – for he recognised the figure as that of a woman who was still alive, as far as he knew: Mrs Juliana Porter, a patient of his whom he had treated for severe depression, or 'melancholia', as it was termed in Victorian times.

"Mrs Porter?" Wallace managed, beholding the startling light-blue aura around the woman, who was now hovering over his desk with raised arms.

"It is I, doctor," said the apparition, "and I have returned to thank you for your help over the years. Please tell my husband and children I am sorry for leaving them this way. And tell my husband to find someone to love him as I did when I was alive."

The ghost then bid him goodbye, turned in mid-air and drifted back out through the closed window. Dr Wallace ran over to see it depart. He opened the window and below him was a policeman in a winter cape, gazing up at the levitating spectre with an expression as shocked as his own. On the other side of the road, an emaciated mongrel dog snapped at the nocturnal airborne visitant. The policeman stood for a while watching the starry skies as if he thought the ghost might return, but the phantom had dissolved into the ether.

"I'm glad you saw her too," shouted down Wallace, but the policeman just shook his head and dutifully continued on his beat.

At ten o'clock that night, another local doctor named Hughes called at Wallace's home to inform him that his patient, Mrs Julian Porter, had committed suicide earlier in the evening at her home at 7 Cadogan Street, Toxteth Park. She had hanged herself from the staircase rails and left a note for her husband, which read: 'I cannot assist you as I should like to, and I feel that I am a burden to you. You have been very good to me, and I have no fault to find with you, but everybody knows that I cannot do my duty to you as I should like.'

So it was true, he really had seen a ghost. Dr Wallace wasted no time in offering his condolences to the Porter family. He also told the dead woman's husband about the ghostly visitation, which had taken place just minutes after the suicide act, and of the ghost's message – for Mr Porter to look after the children and find love again. It is not known if Mr Porter eventually acted on his wife's selfless advice, but he broke down when Wallace conveyed the message from beyond, and said, "No one could ever take her place."

Dr John Wallace was visited a second time by a ghostly visitor two years later, in the August of 1888. On this occasion, he was once again in the study of his Gambier Terrace home, during the evening, as before. This time the apparition came as he was searching for a particular book amongst his vast collection of leather-bound volumes pertaining to medicine, diseases and anatomy. The doctor suddenly stopped what he was doing, because he had the eerie feeling that someone was standing behind him. He turned round to find an alarming figure standing on the other side of the room, close to the wall. A woman of about sixty-something, with wild straggly long grey hair and a hollow-cheeked face, dressed in a long black one-piece robe. Her eyes were bloodshot and glowed with a faint orange light.

Dr Wallace drew back in shock, upon which the woman vanished before his eyes. The instant she vanished, a framed photograph of the doctor's wife, standing on his desk, fell face down. Dr Wallace was a completely rational man, and yet he had the strange foreboding that something momentous was about to happen to his wife. At the time, forty-five-year-old Margaret Gemmel Young Wallace, was holidaying with relatives in Wales, but when she returned the next day, something odd happened. The incident occurred in the dining room, just before eight in the evening. Mrs Wallace was about to sit down to dinner when her chair flew backwards, as if an invisible hand had pulled it from under her. There is an old Irish superstition which says that a person's chair tilting over and falling backwards is a sure omen of imminent death, and one of the servants present, Mary MacMahon, knew of this sign. Dr Wallace later overheard Mary telling another maid about the chair omen, and how she now feared for "m'lady" as she called Mrs Wallace.

On the next day, a Sunday, Mrs Wallace suddenly became quite ill whilst at the breakfast table. Dr Wallace watched in horror as his wife slumped to the floor and all of the life seemed to drain out of her. He sent two servants to fetch Dr Johnson of Canning Street and Dr Harrison, who lived a few doors away. The two doctors arrived, and fought in vain for almost two hours to resuscitate Mrs Wallace, but the spark of life could not be revived and John Wallace's beloved wife passed away from some mysterious condition.

Dr Wallace later learned that the woman in black who had briefly materialised in his study was a type of Welsh banshee, who had haunted his late wife's Welsh family for generations, and her appearances had invariably symbolised an impending death.

MARY DOWN THE GRID

A long time ago, in Edwardian times, the little girls of Scotland Road would sing a curious street rhyme as they played their skipping games:

> *Down the grid where the water goes,*
> *You can see Mary washing her clothes.*
> *Poor little Mary was just a kid.*
> *Mary Mack died down the grid.*

The surface of our city is prone to restless change, but subterranean Liverpool has stayed more or less intact for a hundred years, and this is certainly the case with the city's sewers. A modern grid now exists in the very same place on Scotland Road where Edwardian children once peered down, out of morbid curiosity, through a cast iron grid to the home of Mary Mack. To date, no one knows whether Mary was just a legend, or whether some tragic incident lay behind the rhyme, but for many decades that grid had a reputation for being haunted.

In November 1883, eight-year-old boy Billy Skellets, of 9 Nightingale Square, Hopwood Street, off Scotland Road, set off to play with his friends down by the Leeds and Liverpool Canal. The small gang eventually ended up back on Scotland Road, where Billy wandered off on his own. A girl of seven named Annie Smith saw him peering down the infamous grid associated with Mary

Mack and warned him to stay away from it, or he'd see the horrible ghost. The boy said she was silly, and deliberately peered down the grid out of bravado. A shopkeeper came out of his store and told the boy to keep away from it, because it gave off a terrible stench and all sorts of diseases were to be had from it. An ashen-face Billy turned to the shopkeeper saying that he had just seen the horrible face of a woman down the grid, and she had told him he was going to die. He became very upset and set off home.

Next day, a Friday, Billy Skellets watched a cart trundling down Hopwood Street, bound for Scotland Road. He jumped on it to hitch a ride, as he had done many times before, but this time he lost his footing and fell under one of the huge iron clad wheels, which crushed his head, killing him instantly. On hearing of the tragedy, the shopkeeper on Scotland Road shuddered, recalling the strange prediction the deceased boy had told him the day before. Billy had also told his mother the same terrible story and now she was left to rue the fact that she had dismissed it as a bit of childish fantasising.

~

In July 1884, beautiful thirteen-year-old Mary Ann McConnell, of Slade Street, just a stone's throw from Scotland Road, went to visit her aunt, about a quarter of a mile from her home. It was a blazing hot day, and the girl's aunt sent her for a bottle of lemonade to a shop on Scotland Road. As Mary Ann walked down the famous thoroughfare, she noticed a group of children kneeling around the so-called haunted grid, and decided she'd go and see what was going on. One of the young lads

165

thought he had spied a gold ring down the grid, so he was trying to fish for it with a fishing hook and twine tied to a stick, but he was having no luck. As the children looked on, a grotesque and evil-looking face stared up at them from the sediment of filth beyond the iron bars. The shrunken female face had a greenish caste, and was fringed by a head of dark wet straggly hair. It shrieked out an unintelligible word, before a bony little hand seized the fishing line and dragged it down, yanking the stick out the child's hand.

All the children recoiled in horror, and many of the adult passers-by grinned at their hysterics. No doubt some of them believed they had seen nothing more frightening than a sewer rat – but the shopkeeper who had heard about the sightings of Mary Mack down the grid (including the one from the late Billy Skellets) ran out of his store to find Mary Ann McConnell gazing down the infamous grid with a look of sheer terror etched on her young features. This time the shopkeeper also saw something moving down the grid, but as he bent down to get a closer look it sank beneath the murky foul-smelling water.

The shopkeeper warned Mary Ann to stay well away from the grid because people had caught nasty diseases from the putrid air it gave off, but the girl was back the next day with her friend Ann, who lived in nearby Hornby Street. Both girls arrived at the grid each day and would proceed to taunt the wizened apparition and also cause groups of other children to congregate around it. In the end a policeman had to disband the gang and send the girls away.

That August, the naked body of Mary Ann McConnell was found floating in the Liverpool and Leeds Canal. She had been raped and strangled. Her killer was never

166

brought to justice. Then, in September 1884, the nude and molested body of Ann Pollard, the girl who had peered down the accursed grid on Scotland Road alongside Mary Ann, was also found floating in the Leeds and Liverpool Canal. The police never established whether the same killer had murdered both girls, but it seems highly likely. No one was ever brought to justice for the crimes. Josiah Owens, a flatman working on the canal, was briefly suspected of being implicated in Pollard's death, but was eventually eliminated from the inquiry.

In 1970, one of my readers, Charlie Johnson, lived off Scotland Road. One day he was playing with a 'superball' – a small ball, about four centimetres in diameter, made of an incredibly bouncy ultra-elastic compound known by the trademarked name, Zectron. Superballs were one of the big fads of the Seventies, and it was a common sight to see children bouncing them as high as the rooftops. After bouncing for hundreds of yards down Scotland Road, eleven-year-old Charlie's superball came to rest, lodged precariously between the bars of the 'haunted' grid.

As Charlie went to retrieve it, a small slender finger and thumb grabbed at it and pulled it down into the grid. Someone was down there, and Charlie ran to his cousin's home in nearby Bevington Hill to tell him what had happened, only to have him call him a liar. But the boy's grandmother knew better, and asked him to tell her the exact whereabouts of the grid. "By Harrops the Chemist, Gran," he replied, and his grandmother nodded knowingly and told him how the grid in question was said to be haunted by the ghost of a child named Mary Mack, who was killed by her uncle and stuffed down the grid in Victorian times, and people who saw the spirit down that grid usually met a bad end soon afterwards. Charlie lived in mortal fear of meeting his death for months afterwards, yet he is still alive today!

Is the legend of Mary Down the Grid all coincidence and legend – or does the spirit of a forgotten Victorian murder victim still haunt the drain where she was killed?

JOURNEY INTO TERROR

A few names and minor details have been altered in the following story, which is true and happened exactly as I describe it here.

A few years ago, thirty-two-year-old Martin left a pub in West Derby and, slightly intoxicated, waited by a main road to flag down a taxi. He checked the time on his mobile phone, as he fancied going to the chippy, and it closed at 11.30pm. It was exactly 11pm. The battery level indicator was flashing on the phone screen, and bleeping with annoying regularity, so he switched it off. A creature of habit, Martin left the pub at the same time most nights, and he was pleasantly surprised to see a taxi slowly coming down the road with its golden hire light on. He jumped in, and spouted out an address in the Wavertree area, but didn't close the taxi door properly.

"Could you close that again please, mate?"

"Yeah, sorry," Martin said, and reopened the door and slammed it shut.

The taxi moved off, and the door locks clicked into place. Martin noticed that the taxi driver hadn't started the fare meter, so he told him to. The cabby slowly poked the button on the meter with his index finger and then looked in his rear-view mirror at Martin for a while, making him feel a little uneasy.

"Good game today, mate, eh?" Martin said, referring

to the football match that saw LFC hammer Manchester United. The driver said nothing.

"Oh, are you a blue then?" Martin remarked, beaming a false grin. He then noticed the long pigtail of coppery-grey hair, hanging from the back of the cabby's bald head.

The vehicle began to accelerate steadily. Taxis always seemed to move faster at night, but Martin had read somewhere that it was just a nocturnal illusion. He continued trying to make small talk, but the man behind the wheel kept quiet.

Exasperated with his rudeness, Martin swore and said, "What's up? Is your intercom broken, mate?"

No reply – just the occasional meeting of his eyes with the cabby's steely eyes in the rear-view mirror.

When he did finally speak, it was to casually ask, "Are you ready to die?"

"What?"

"I said ... are you ready to die?"

"Are you on drugs or something, mate?" Then Martin leaned forward and through the gap in the Perspex window, snapped, "Pull over."

Instead, the taxi charged forward in a burst of acceleration, and Martin was flung backwards on to the floor. He was now stone cold sober, and his heart was pounding.

The hackney cab flashed by the street in the Wavertree suburbs where Martin lived and sped on towards Picton Road. Within a minute the hackney was flying past Wavertree Road police station at over eighty miles per hour and then jumped the traffic lights at the Overton Street junction. The cab was travelling so fast, it almost failed to make the bend on Irvine Street and

170

practically mounted the pavement near the Mount Vernon pub. Here the taxi slowed before turning on to Crown Street and then Brownlow Hill. Meanwhile Martin was frantically trying to dial 999 on his mobile phone, but the battery had failed and the phone screen kept briefly lighting up then going out. By now the taxi was rocketing down Hanover Street.

"Stop this cab, I've called the police!" Martin yelled at the suicidal cabby.

"Too late for the police, Martin," said the driver. "You'd do better calling the coroner."

What did he mean? Just what did this crazed cabby intend to do with him?

"We're going into the Canning Dock. You ready?" the taxi driver suddenly announced.

Martin tried to open the doors but the safety locks were on. He pulled off his shoe and tried to smash the side windows with the heel but didn't even manage to crack the pane. He tried to open the electric windows by repeatedly jabbing the 'down' arrow button – but they wouldn't budge.

The driver turned to face his terrified passenger, who was now on his knees, close to tears, "You should have stayed away from Claire McGee!"

In a flash it hit Martin. The married woman he'd been seeing every Thursday – Claire. This had to be some relation of hers out for revenge.

"Oh, my god! I give you my word I'll never go near her again!"

But the cabby ignored his pleas, "Better take a deep breath, here's the Canning Dock!" he said, and turned to grin at Martin, who was about to throw up.

The taxi crossed a central reservation, and the impact

threw Martin into the air. Then he accelerated down Wapping and swerved towards the cobbled quayside.

Martin let out a scream – and found himself curled up in the foetal position about six feet from the edge of the Canning Dock. His shirt front was drenched with vomit and he lay there, completely disorientated. Unsteadily he got to his feet, expecting to see a mass of froth and bubbles in the dock, where the hackney had gone in, but the waters were as still as a mirror, not a ripple in sight.

Martin staggered off in a daze, wearing only one shoe, unable to make any sense of what had happened. As he made his way up Water Street a hackney cab slowed down for him. The cabby looked him up and down, assuming he'd been out on the town and wanted to get home, "Come on then, mate. Get in."

But Martin froze, frightened the demonic taxi driver had returned. It took him over an hour and twenty minutes in his socks to reach his home in Wavertree, where he sat all night, drinking coffee, going over the inexplicable incident in his mind. He phoned his best friend Dave, who coincidentally happened to be a cabbie. He knocked off work at 3am and went straight round to Martin's home. Dave sat there deep in thought for a while after Martin had repeated his story a second time, and then said, "It's odd how he knew your name, isn't it?"

"What do you mean?"

"Well, you said that he said, 'Too late for the police, Martin, you'd be better calling the coroner.'"

"Ah, yes, you're right … he did."

David took off his spectacles, polished them with a handkerchief, then said, "Claire McGee had a brother-in-law named Frank ... he was on the hackneys. He died at the wheel. Don't you remember that case ... it was a few years ago now?"

"No," Martin replied, not liking what he was hearing.

"Yeah, he died suddenly from er ... what was that condition ... yeah, ventricular fibrillation ... because of an undiagnosed heart condition. His brother's Terry McGee – Claire's husband."

"What did Frank McGee look like? Can you remember?" Martin recalled the odd little pigtail that the cabby had sported from the nape of his neck.

"I think I only ever saw him twice," Dave admitted.

"Do you know if he had a pony tail?"

"He was bald."

"So was this guy," said Martin.

Dave said he would ask around, and true to his word, he telephoned Martin later that evening.

"Yeah, you were right, me mates said he did have a pony tail. It was sort of red with grey in it."

Martin went cold. The image of the freaky cabby and his weird little rat's tail seared forever on his brain.

He stuck to his promise – he didn't dare do otherwise – and never saw Claire McGee again, nor would he get into a hackney cab for some time after that terrifying night journey.

What are we to make of this story? If it is true, then Frank McGee somehow returned from beyond the grave, perhaps to teach Martin a lesson for committing adultery with his brother's wife? Believe it or not, the annals of the paranormal are crammed with well-documented reports of phantom cars, ships and other inanimate, 'soulless' objects. An empty, driverless phantom bus has

173

been seen for many years, tearing down Mulgrave Street and Grove Street in the wee small hours with its headlights blazing, long after the bus services have ceased. In the mid-1930s a phantom red double-decker bus was often seen travelling at great speed through Kensington, London. The ghost bus caused so many accidents, many of them fatal, that residents who lived in the vicinity of the hauntings wrote to the newspapers. Even a respected transport official saw the double-decker pull into his depot and vanish before his eyes.

Another apparently inanimate ghost is the spectral 'Devil's Coach' which has been seen trundling along the roads of Childwall, Allerton and Wavertree at all hours of the morning. So, it would seem that the world of apparitions is not confined to human beings; inanimate objects can also haunt us – perhaps even a ghost in a spectral hackney.

~

On the warm Saturday morning of 23 June 1973, sixty-year-old John Stafford was laid up in bed with a bad case of the flu, as his wife of forty years, Gladys, painted his feet with an anti-fungal compound called Gentian Violet. She then propped up John's four duck feather pillows and switched on the portable black and white television for him. At his bedside was the usual box of tissues, pot of Vick's vapour rub, tube of Dequadin throat lozenges and a bottle of Lucozade. Anyway, John blew his nose and then lay back to watch *Sesame Street*, followed by an Australian children's drama called *Catch Kandy*. He then got out of bed, turned the television off, and decided to listen to some music. He took his old Murphy record

174

player from the top of the wardrobe and tried to find his old Bing Crosby 78s, but they were nowhere to be seen. He found a stack of 45rpm singles that had belonged to his son and loaded them on to the record player.

The effort made him feel a bit groggy, so he got back into bed, and sank into the pillows. He drifted off as the first single, 'Good Timin' by Jimmy Jones, began. Then something very odd happened. John started to dream that he was back in the sixties, and it was what is known as a lucid dream – a dream where the dreamer is aware that he's actually asleep. He pinched himself on the wrist, and it hurt. He should have woken up, but he didn't. He also noticed his flu symptoms had gone, and he could breathe perfectly well. He looked around and found himself in a street that no longer exists – Cases Street, which used to run from Ranelagh Street to Clayton Square. John walked into a tobacconists next door to a pub called the Globe, and asked a woman, "What year is this?"

The woman narrowed her eyes at him, assuming he was drunk, or barmy, then said, "You really don't know what year it is?"

John swore he didn't, and the bemused tobacconist said, "Well, it's 1966, love," and seemed as though she was waiting for John to come back with the punch line of some joke.

John walked out of the tobacconists and pinched himself again. He was perplexed, and yet he felt so young; definitely not like a man of sixty. He looked at his reflection in a shop window and was taken aback to find that he was someone he had never seen before in his life. He had blond hair in a quiff, very reminiscent of the singer Rory Storm, and wore a suede donkey jacket, dark shirt, drainpipe jeans and ankle-length boots. In his pocket he found a wallet containing five pound notes, and an assortment of pre-decimal coins, but no driver's licence, or any documents that might have his name on.

John strolled into the Mecca cafe on Clayton Square and ordered a coffee to steady his nerves. A stunning girl of about seventeen or eighteen was sitting at a table on her own. She lit a cigarette and looked at him as she slowly exhaled. In front of her was a half-eaten sandwich and a cup of tea. John asked if he could join her, and sat down before she could say no.

"Hi, how you doin'?" he said, trying to sound casual.

The girl wasn't sure what to make of him at first, but she was very taken with his pop starish appearance and anyway the place was full of people and he seemed friendly and genuine. John's fear subsided and he started chatting quite naturally to the girl, who revealed that her name was Gwen Appleton and that she worked in a nearby shop on Church Street. She often came to the Mecca during her lunch break.

Then John dropped the bombshell, "I know this sounds stupid, but is this really 1966?"

"Are you having me on, or what? Course it is, what year did you think it was?"

"Well that's the trouble, you see … I … I don't really know."

John went on to admit that he didn't know who he was, never mind what year it was. Gwen quickly concluded that he was suffering from amnesia, and advised him to go to the nearest hospital. John found himself really falling for Gwen, and he had no wish to scare her away by admitting that he was really a man of sixty from 1973, so he went along with the idea of suffering memory loss. Gwen offered to go with him to the Royal Hospital, but John thanked her and said he'd rather go by himself.

"Okay, I'll meet you after I've finished work … that's if you want to …" said the girl.

"Yeah … yeah I'd love that," said John, trying not to sound too eager but grinning from ear to ear.

"I'll meet you outside Cooper's Cafe at half-past four then. See you later."

For three and a half hours John tramped the streets of 1966 Liverpool, and at one point, went into the Wimpy snack bar on Lime Street to get something to eat. When he came out he realised he was being followed by two men in black leather jackets, both aged about twenty-five. As he turned the corner by the Vines pub, on to Copperas Hill, the men suddenly sprinted after him. He got as far as the Ribble Bus Garage, when one of the pursuers grabbed him by his jacket collar and swung him round. He was punched in the nose and eye, then hit the ground stunned.

"That's off McMullen!" said his assailant.

John suddenly woke up in bed in agony. His nose was bleeding, and when Gladys his wife came in she noticed that his eye was swollen. A doctor was sent for but ignored all his talk about the realistic dream, saying he had probably fallen out of bed.

A week later, whilst Gladys was visiting her sister, John lay on his bed and put the record player on, and once again he found himself back in the same dream, only this time he was standing outside Coopers, anxiously waiting to meet Gwen. His parallel dream-life with Gwen continued and John became so wrapped up in it, that Gladys feared for his sanity and one day when he was

177

pottering about at his allotment, she got someone to take the old record player and his collection of forty-fives away. That did the trick, and John Stafford never encountered Gwen Appleton in his dreams again, and eventually thanked his wife for rescuing him from a sinister, though he had to admit pleasurable, separate life.

He died in 2003 aged eighty.

CATHODE DREAMS

Today there are hundreds of satellite, cable and terrestrial channels that cater for the interests of most television viewers, but some readers may recall the days when the UK only had BBC1, ITV and BBC2 (which began broadcasting in April 1964). Channel 4 was later transmitted into our homes in November 1982. In those days, the four television stations usually ceased their transmissions between midnight and 1am, and a man would appear before 'Closedown' and say something like: "Have a peaceful night, and remember to switch off your television set; goodnight." All the transmitters would then go off air, and in the absence of any signals, 'white noise' would be emitted from the screen of any television that happened to be switched on.

In these days of perpetual television transmission, it is rare to see the speckled pattern associated with white noise on our screens, but on Thursday, 28 January 1982, something was seen in the white noise of a television set that sparked off a strange episode for two teenaged girls. The girls were fourteen-year-old Heather Smith and her best friend Judy, who was staying over at Heather's home on a certain stretch of Queen's Drive. The girls sat up in bed, munching cheese-flavoured 'Wotsits' and sweet chewy 'Arrow Bars', as they watched an episode of the television series 'Tenspeed and Brownshoe' (starring a young Jeff Goldblum). When the programme ended, the girls talked about anything and everything until Granada television closed down. Then the white noise came on the screen. Judy was propped up against the headboard, gazing at the blizzard of static, when a woman's face suddenly appeared. The smiling face kept on coming nearer until Judy recognised it, "Hey, look, it's Mrs Moore!"

Heather confirmed that it was definitely the beautiful Linda Moore, who used to teach English at the girl's school. What was she doing on the television? They turned the volume up but could hear nothing except a loud hissing sound, like an amplified waterfall, so they quickly turned it back down to a faint level, before it woke the entire household. A man's face then appeared in the screen, applying shaving foam to his chin. The girls both gasped in unison, as they recognised the face of the man who lived next door – Mr Durban – a man with a rather supercilious face who bore a strong resemblance to the actor Bernard Cribbins. He carried on shaving, and the girls were baffled as to how they could see him and Mrs Moore on the television at nearly two o'clock in the morning, and couldn't take their eyes off the intriguing images on the screen. Mrs Moore reappeared and her face came very close to the screen as she closed her eyes and puckered her lips, as if about to kiss someone. She kissed the screen, and Judy and Heather giggled at the bizarre sight, especially when Mrs Moore said, "Is this wrong, David?" Her voice clearly audible over the hiss of the static.

Judy then recalled that David was Mr Durban's Christian name. The girls gradually started putting two and two together – incredibly, it seemed that David Durban, Heather's married next door neighbour, was having an affair with Mrs Moore. The girls remained rooted to the screen, engrossed in the ghostly images.

Then David Durban's voice came through the television speaker. "No, this isn't wrong, Linda; I love you and you love me, so let them all go to hell. They wish they had love like this!"

Then the scene changed, and now Mrs Moore's head was lying on a pillow. Mr Durban talked to her about meeting up at a bar on Lark Lane, to which Mrs Moore responded, "But what are we going to do about your wife?"

With a grim smile, Mr Durban whispered that he planned to go on a winter hike up Snowdon with his wife, and he would take her up the Llanberis Path, where lots of walkers had lost their lives over the years. "A little push and …!" The girls shuddered as the image changed to a woman falling down a snowy slope and smashing into crags after a sheer drop. The screen went blank again and there were no more images that night.

On the following morning Heather Smith told her mother what they had seen, but her mum reckoned they had just tuned into a film that had been picked up from a distant station, that's all. The girls were convinced there was more to it than that, so they went to a public phone box down the road, and through directory enquiries, obtained Mr Durban's number. Mrs Durban answered, and without any preamble, Heather warned her that her husband was planning to push her off Snowdon because he was having an affair with Mrs Moore, an English teacher. Mrs Durban was furious at what she took to be a cruel hoax and hung up. At that moment, who should Judy notice but Mr Durban, standing outside right by the telephone box, and her heart somersaulted, but he had just stopped to light a cigarette and was using the booth to shield it from the wind. He moved on without glancing at the terrified girls.

That night, Judy was allowed to stay over at Heather's home again, and at 10pm both girls pinned their ears to the wall when a terrific row broke out next door, which ended in Mr Durban being told to get out. The police arrived, and Mr Durban assured them that everything was okay, he was leaving.

The next day, Heather Smith's mother said she had just been talking to a distraught Mrs Durban, who had told her that she was going to divorce her husband. She had followed him from his workplace to a wine bar on Lark Lane, where he sat holding hands with Linda Moore, the woman the girls had seen in the white noise of the television set. Mrs Smith couldn't bring herself to believe the girls' far-fetched story, yet she had no other way of explaining how they had obtained the knowledge about Durban's affair.

There is a possibility that the random pattern of speckles that made up the white noise pattern on the cathode ray tube of Heather's television screen were being affected by the power of David Durban's unconscious mind as he slept in the house next door to Heather's. The history of the paranormal is full of cases featuring the phenomenon of psychokinesis – also called telekinesis – the movement of objects and substances through the radiation of an unknown power by the mind. There have been cases I know of personally where people have found strange-looking orbs and other unexplained anomalies in the images taken on a digital camera in the company of a certain person – who was actually imprinting images from his subconscious mind on to the digital photographs. These orbs and other visual 'irregularities' captured in the photographs were thought to be ghosts and other forms of spirit manifestation, but I soon realised that the images only occurred in cameras when a certain person was present. Computers, mobile phones, iPods and other electrical devices would always malfunction in the presence of this same person.

Perhaps our philandering Mr Durban was one of these psychic 'lighthouses' who send out their thoughts, and in some cases, the psychic emanations somehow modulate the electrons in things like a cathode ray tube of the type used in Heather's television set of 1982. In other words, what Heather and Judy were actually seeing were Mr Durban's dreams via the television through a form of unconscious telekinesis.

LABOUR PAINS

The sharp mingled scent of petrol, diesel, Senior Service cigarette smoke, hot tar and sea salt spray were ever-present in the summer air over Liverpool's Mann Island that sun-baked morning in the early 1970s. The cream and black liveried Crossville coach, bound for London, began to admit passengers at the bus stop next to the Dock Board building. Amongst the long-distance travellers was thirty-five-year-old, worldly-wise, Huytonian Tony Brooks; wide-boy, womaniser, wit … In fact, a bit of 'a case', as we used to say in those days. Randomly, Tony ended up sitting next to his exact opposite: the virginal Roy Scott, twenty-five years of age and living at home with his mum and aunt in the Dingle; a simple man who had never been drunk and sorely missed the family cat Vinnie whenever he went to stay with his cousin Bill Berry down in the big metropolis.

Well, this green-as-grass young man found himself sitting next to Tony Brooks throughout the seven-hour journey, and by the time the Crossville pulled into Victoria Coach Station, Brooks had the impressionable Dingle lad enthralled with his tales. It all started when Roy noticed the unusual golden ring, adorned with a skull, worn by Tony. "Can you read what it says around it?" Tony had asked, thrusting the ring close to Roy's eyes. Roy could just make out the five words engraved in a semi-circular banner above the grinning skull: 'As You

Were, I Was' – and on the curved banner under the jaw of the golden face of death, were the chilling words: 'As I Am – You Shall Be'.

"That's a bit morbid, isn't it?" mumbled Roy, slightly upset by the message.

Tony gritted his teeth, then said, "True though, ain't it, lad? And we only come this way once, so grab life with both hands before it's too late."

First port of call was a pub on Shaftesbury Avenue, where Tony paid for the first drink, and Roy paid for everything else from then on. "You got a Judy back home then?" Tony queried, then hid his smirk behind an upturned glass of Gordon's gin. A bleary-eyed, hiccuping Roy replied with an uncertain nod. He'd never even been kissed by a girl in reality, but he daren't admit that in front of Tony, who bragged how he'd been with all the "good-time girls of Paris, Hamburg, Liverpool and London".

Then the two men made their way, in an alcoholic haze, to a strip club off Wardour Street, but they were too drunk to get past the Welsh doorman, so they wandered down a backstreet, and it was there that a wild-looking foreign woman with curly hair, suddenly stepped out of a pub doorway and said, "Tony?" A second, older woman of the night, probably the wrong side of fifty, slunk out of the backstreet pub. Tony later explained that the younger woman was 'Melody Mint' and her older friend was a strange woman who read Tarot cards for a living. Her name was Magdala.

"So, this is Tony, is it?" Magdala remarked to Melody flashing a look of disgust towards the Huytonian. Tony swore at Melody and called her revolting names as he tried to get away, but he was very unsteady on his feet, as was Roy. "I'm having your child, Tony," Melody said in a tearful voice, with her hands on the scarcely concealed large bump under her flowing dress. "That's a lie!" Tony screamed, upon which Magdala declared, "Couvade upon you!" pointing at the Huyton man. Used to extracting himself from tight situations, Tony stuck his fingers in his mouth and power-whistled a taxi. Magdala looked deranged, and he hadn't got a clue what she was going on about – but he soon would …

The taxi, driven by a comical Arthur English lookalike, quickly left the neon jungle of Soho behind, and as the vehicle rattled round a badly-lit corner to the Goldhawk Road, towards the home of Roy Scott's cousin in Shepherd's Bush, Tony Brooks yelled out, "Me haversack! Turn back." He'd suddenly realised he had dropped his haversack in that Soho alleyway in his rush to get away from Melody and Magdala. All it contained was a towel, toothbrush, 'Pagan Man' aftershave, two shirts, his beloved pair of bottle-green flared 'kecks', a can of 'Aqua Manda' hairspray (purloined from his teenaged sister), a pair of sunglasses and a flick-comb. To the cabby, young Roy Scott shouted, "We can't afford to go back, just continue to Sycamore Gardens please!"

Tony clenched his teeth and his right fist, placing the latter menacingly under Roy's chin. The infantile and intoxicated Roy reached into his own haversack, withdrew a chocolate bar, and offered it to Tony, but the tough guy angrily shook his head and tears rolled down Roy's face. "What a night!" he sobbed and reclined back, crestfallen, into the padded seat. The cabdriver was paid, and Roy found himself instantly skint. He hammered on the front door of cousin Bill Berry's home, unaware that the time was now 3.05am. With relief, Roy and Tony noticed a dim orange light filter from the inner vestibule

186

door, then listened to the bolt being drawn back. Billy, a bearded man of forty, sporting spectacles, Y-fronts and a white Keep Britain Tidy tee-shirt, opened the door. He glared first at Roy, and then at Tony.

"Oh my God! What've we got 'ere? Rolf Harris or what?" said Tony.

"And who're you, you cheeky beggar?"

Despite his travelling companion's rudeness, Roy begged his cousin to let him stay with them – just for one night. "I know he's a bit a rough diamond, Billy, but his heart's in the right place, isn't that right, Tony?"

Tony just shrugged, but Bill reluctantly agreed, probably sensing trouble if he refused.

The three men stayed up all that night, and Roy and Tony sampled Bill's home-brewed ale. At 5am, Tony Brooks suddenly cried out in agony, doubled up, then fell to the floor, clutching his stomach. He managed to sit up shortly afterwards, and Bill said he'd phone for an ambulance but Tony said he was alright. "Just wind," he joked. He went to the toilet minutes later, and let out a scream. Bill had to charge at the lavatory door to gain entry, and inside, he found Tony lying prostrate in the bath staring in disbelief at what was now his unnaturally huge domed stomach; just like the abdomen of a heavily pregnant woman. He jabbered out something about his belly swelling up before his eyes – and now he could feel something kicking inside the swelling!

Bill rushed downstairs to phone an ambulance and one arrived soon afterwards. The paramedic, with a half-grin and suspicious eye, went to the bathroom, to find that there was indeed a man exhibiting all the signs of imminent childbirth. Tony cried out in agony intermittently, as though he were having contractions,

187

and tried to push out whatever was in his stomach, but it wouldn't budge. He was taken to hospital, and at half-past five that morning, he let out a spine-chilling scream which must have woken every patient in the hospital, and though no baby appeared, his overblown belly slowly collapsed.

Three months later, Tony visited his new mate Roy at his Dingle home and told him he had recently received a letter from Magdala in which she said she had found the haversack he had dropped, and had extracted a single hair of his from the comb in that bag. That hair was all she needed in order to cast a 'couvade spell'. Couvade is a well-reported phenomenon by which a man psychically, though just as painfully, shares the childbirth and labour pains of the woman he has made pregnant.

On the morning Tony's stomach had deflated, at precisely 5.30am, Melody had given birth to a baby daughter ...

THE PIPER

One grey afternoon in November 1965, as the BBC's Saturday Bandstand programme blared out an optimistic tune on his Dansette radio, sixty-five-year-old Jack Owens of Everton decided to kill himself in a rather unusual way. In an effort to induce a fatal heart attack, he repeatedly ran up and down two flights of stairs at his home off Netherfield Road South, until he fell to his knees from the bottom step, wheezing with empty lungs. With volcanic anger he pounded the cheap old dusty carpet on the hallway floor with his fist. "Why?" he gasped, "Why? Why? Why?" and his desperate cries caught in his throat, as he thought of his beloved late wife Theresa, who had passed away from cancer, and now Jack yearned to be with her once again. He felt he had nothing left to live for, and although he had been assured by many people that time was a great healer, he found that all the sweet memories of the life he had known with his soul-mate were now nothing but wound-openers.

Suddenly there was a knock at the door; probably yet another caring neighbour trying to cheer me up and save me, he thought bitterly. "Go away!" Jack warned them, but a faint familiar voice replied, "Uncle Jack? It's me … Millie."

It was the thirteen-year-old niece he loved – and she reminded him so much of his late wife in both her ways and looks. Jack quickly picked himself up off the hallway floor, took several deep breaths to regain his equilibrium, and with a deep sigh answered the door. Millie came in brightly, clutching her recorder, and Jack staggered into the kitchen to switch off the radio. The girl was like a fresh summer zephyr on this gloomy autumnal afternoon, and she breezed into the terraced house, playing the recorder as she skipped down the hall into the parlour. Jack wondered if her parents had been fighting again, and he asked her if everything was alright. She nodded as she picked out the notes of 'When the Saints Go Marching In'.

"Are you sure you're alright?" Jack asked again, and Millie stopped playing the recorder and replied with a Jimmy Clitheroe catchphrase: "Aye, I'm all there with me cough drops."

Uncle and niece watched professional wrestling on the television for a while, and then Millie went out to see a friend at that local rocky playground called Whitley Gardens. The friend was a gooey-eyed lad named Rory who had a crush on her, and he watched spellbound as she sat perched on a sandstone rock in the playground, playing her recorder. November darkness was falling fast, and in the twilight, Rory heard something eerie. Whenever Millie stopped playing, faint flute music would be heard somewhere in the distance.

"Don't be daft … you're hearing things," Millie told her admirer, but then she too heard the strains of the uncanny melody floating on the wind. A full moon rising over Gregson Street was not helping matters either. Millie played the first eight notes of 'When the Saints Go Marching In', and the unseen recorder player replied with the twenty-three other notes which made up the melody (which happens to be from an old funeral song).

190

Rory was visibly frightened, and said he had to go home, using the excuse of wanting to see the *Dick Emery Show* at eight o'clock. He walked Millie to Shaw Street, then hurried off home to Roscommon Street.

Millie, now a little scared herself, turned the corner and walked down Prince Edwin Street, which was thankfully busy, being an early Saturday evening. However, as she passed an alleyway she caught a glimpse of a man lurking there in a flat cap. There was something very unpleasant about his face, which even seen fleetingly, seemed to be brimming with menace, and he too was playing a recorder. For some reason, Millie instantly knew that she was looking at the Devil himself and his presence cast an invisible shadow of ancient pure fear over her.

Millie hurried down Prince Edwin Street, afraid to steal even one more glance at the primeval trickster, but she could hear his clip-clop gait following close behind – the unmistakable sound of his hooves. She was tormented by the thought of his pointed ears, sinister black rimmed eyes and long aquiline nose. He began to play the recorder and it was the sound she had heard earlier in Whitley Gardens. The melody was, as Millie would later discover, 'The Carnival is Over' – a song by The Seekers, her favourite pop group; a song that hadn't been released yet, but its melody was based on an old Russian folk song entitled 'Stenka Razin'. The music stopped abruptly as Millie approached her Uncle Jack's house, and in a low refined voice the Devil said, "Tell Uncle Jack I'm here. Tell him I'll consider his offer."

Millie still wouldn't turn to face the Devil, and she hammered on her uncle's door, but she could still see him out of the corner of her eye, standing under an unlit

191

lamppost. As soon as Uncle Jack came to the door, reeking of whisky, Millie barged in and slammed the door shut behind her. She couldn't get her words out at first, but she managed to tell her uncle about the weird man outside and how he'd followed her from the park. Then she relayed the Devil's cryptic message, about Jack considering the offer, though she had no idea of its meaning. Her words sobered Jack immediately, together with the tell-tale silhouette of the Father of All Lies on the parlour blinds. "I didn't mean it! Go away!" he shouted.

"Didn't mean what?" asked Millie, holding on to his arm, trembling.

"I said an idiotic thing earlier, just after you left. I wasn't thinking straight." Jack looked so petrified, his fear rubbed off on Millie, as she'd never seen him like that. "I was desperate, and stupidly agreed to give my soul to the Devil if I could only see my Theresa again," Jack admitted, and covered his head with his hands. "What have I done? Oh! What have I done?" he moaned.

"May I come in?" came a loud rich voice close by.

This time the Devil was peering out of the mirror over the fireplace. Uncle Jack screamed, "No!" and Millie began to cry. The olive green face grimaced and somehow spat on the inside of the mirror before vanishing. Jack and Millie stood without stirring for a very long time, until they were sure Beelzebub had definitely gone.

They slowly began to regain their composure, but it had affected them both deeply. Then came a soft miaowing; it was a tiny little tabby kitten on the pavement outside, crying as though it had been abandoned by its mother. Millie instinctively opened the front door, just a crack, looked both ways, then bent down to scoop up the defenceless little creature, even

192

though Uncle Jack eyed it with suspicion and repeatedly said, "No, Millie. Leave it there!"

Then he and Millie once again saw the Devil standing on the other side of the street in a shadowy doorway, watching them. He shouted something and walked towards them, so Jack and Millie, who was clutching the kitten, slammed the front door shut.

In the back parlour Jack put on the television, as a distraction from the terrifying situation. After the little black and white television, with its goldfish bowl screen had warmed up, Benny Hill's comical face appeared – just what was needed to diffuse the menace that seemed to have followed them indoors. Every light in the house was switched on, and an hour passed without sight or sound of Satan.

Then came screams from Millie. A sneering monochrome face on the television glared right at her and said, "May I come in now?"

Jack ripped the television's plug from the wall socket.

"Oh! I give up, goodbye!" came a disembodied voice from the unplugged television.

At midnight, Millie's worried parents called at Uncle Jack's house, and a white faced Millie let them in and wordlessly pointed to Uncle Jack lying dead on the kitchen floor. Natural causes, or the Devil's work?

That same night, at 2am, Millie lay tearfully cradling the kitten in bed until she suddenly realised it had six toes on each paw. "Don't do that!" hissed the kitten, its features contorted into a feline nightmare, as Millie threw it out of the window. She wet herself with fear, and when she pushed back the curtains to look out of the window, there was the Devil again, lying on his back on the pavement, with his legs making cycling movements in the air, laughing demonically to himself.

Millie shrank back from the curtains, and as she did so she heard clumping footsteps on the wall outside. It was the Devil himself running up the vertical wall towards the roof. There was a fluttering sound, and thankfully, that was the last Millie ever heard of the Devil.

CHRISTMAS TIMESLIP

Many of the local slippages of time I have written about, in which people find themselves stepping into the past or future, for some reason have occurred on Bold Street. Here's an account of a journey back to a Victorian Christmas that took place in 1965.

In August of that year, Roger, a trainee doctor, his girlfriend Val, and two veterinary student friends, Harry and Craig, were travelling along Berry Street in Roger's Mini, when the vehicle began to rattle and shake, as if passing over cobblestones. The road, however, looked perfectly normal, so Roger figured there must be something wrong with the Mini's suspension. He turned left into Bold Street, where he and his passengers were shocked to find it was snowing – in the middle of summer! Then Val noticed that all the shops and people looked out of date. Green garlands gemmed with bright red flowers festooned the bow windows with their bull's eye panes. Men in top hats and black hammer coat tails strutted along with walking canes, and the women all wore long dark coats and ankle-length dresses.

At one point the time-displaced Mini was heading straight for a horse-drawn hansom cab, which just veered out of the way in the nick of time, and the driver angrily lashed the vehicle with his whip as the hansom trundled past. Backseat passenger Harry thought Bold Street had been dressed up for some Victorian film set that was being shot – in no other way could he take in and rationalise what was taking place.

Roger pulled over at the junction of Bold Street and Hanover Street, wound down his window, and attempted to ask one of the 'extras' which film was being shot, but it was then that events took a sinister turn. Val noticed a bedraggled barefoot boy of about nine or ten standing in the slushy snow at the kerbside, staring at their car in awe. The boy suddenly turned to his right, and the sound of galloping hooves could be heard. In the rear view mirror, Roger could see two mounted policemen tearing down Bold Street on their steeds. He stalled the car, then managed to start it again and sped down Hanover Street with the antiquated but terrifying Victorian policemen in close pursuit.

The street was crowded with all kinds of carts, pedestrians and men pushing barrows laden with every conceivable type of goods. The road surface beneath all this bustle was slippery and cobbled, unlike Bold Street, which had been thick with snow just minutes before. Val screamed for Roger to get away from the scene as quickly as possible, when, all of a sudden, the surroundings outside returned to normal, bright sunshine replaced the wintry weather. A modern-day Cousins cake shop – a banal sight which they would normally barely notice – confirmed their conviction that they were back in the present day.

THE FUNNYOSITY AND THE ARMY OF
MATCHSTICK MEN

Modern physicists tell us there are dimensions of space and time we know nothing about, and worlds alongside our own which exist on the fringes of what we understand as reality. On the outskirts of our hazy everyday world of personal preoccupations, there lies a greater and far more interesting reality which we sleepwalkers are only able to glimpse now and then. Sometimes the dwellers from these unknown regions are seen by the denizens of this world and are interpreted as ghosts, faeries, demons, vampires or angels. The following bizarre story is a case in point.

At a house on Muirhead Avenue, in 2008, eighteen-year-old Haley was visiting her boyfriend Andrew one dismal rainy afternoon and was waiting in his bedroom as he went downstairs to ask his mother if she could lend him some money. As Haley sat in the room, the door slowly creaked open a few inches, and what initially looked like a puppet peeped around the door. She assumed it was Andrew's nine-year-old brother, Sam, who loved to come and chat to her and show her his toys, but when she looked a bit closer, Haley saw that the puppet was not being worked by anyone. It was very life-like and had a rather sinister appearance. It wore a purple pointed hat and a long black robe, and the beady darting eyes had black lines running beneath them in the style of the old Pierrot pantomime clowns.

"Hello there!" it said, and Haley, out of habit whenever she came across anything unusual, got out her mobile phone and took a picture of the weird puppet.

"No, don't!" the figure said, holding up a tiny hand in protest. Too late – the phone clicked, and the puppet darted back behind the door. Haley didn't dare move, and she shouted at the top of her voice for Andrew, who came bounding up the stairs. He thought she was just winding him up, but then Haley showed him the photograph and he went cold. To date, Haley has not yet plucked up the courage to return to that house on Muirhead Avenue.

~

In 2001 I received a call at the studios of Radio Merseyside after talking about the paranormal on the *Billy Butler Show*. Ann, a seventy-year-old listener, told me how, in 1967, she stayed with her heavily pregnant sister Alice at her home on Stalisfield Avenue, West Derby. One night, Alice's six-year-old son, Anthony, said there was a "little man with a pointy hat" under his bed, and Ann, playing along with the child, asked him what the little man was called. The boy gave a curious reply.

"He said he's a 'Funnyosity', Auntie Ann," Anthony said, quite matter of factly, and dragged her to his bedroom to see the miniature visitor for herself. Ann smiled and went along with the boy's little 'game'. She went into the room and her nephew giggled and said, "Listen, Auntie, he's singing!"

Sure enough, as Ann listened, she heard a barely audible voice singing a song she happened to know:

'What Have They Done to the Rain?' by The Searchers. She felt the hairs on the back of her neck stiffen as she listened to the eerie singing voice coming from beneath the bed, and quickly left the bedroom, dragging her nephew with her. Alice told her sister she'd probably heard a radio playing somewhere, but the Funnyosity could not be explained away so easily.

On the following day in the afternoon, little Anthony trotted into the kitchen where Ann was cooking, and told her a long convoluted story about a woman called Nell Mooney who had sprayed DDT at the Funnyosity and ended up being attacked by him and his "little friends". "She collapsed and died from the fright," Anthony told his aunt gleefully, and also chillingly explained how the Funnyosity couldn't die because he was already dead.

"Where is he now?" Ann asked her nephew.

"He's behind you!" he replied in an excited high-pitched voice. Out of the corner of her eye, Ann caught a glimpse of something doll-like tiptoeing along the draining board. Before she could turn, the thing was gone. After that day, the Funnyosity was seen no more but I have a sneaking suspicion he's still about.

~

In 2007, another strange phenomenon, as inexplicable and mischievous as the Funnyosity, manifested itself in the bedroom of a girl named Kayleigh at her West Derby home. Kayleigh's family had recently moved into the semi-detached house, just a stone's throw from Croxteth Hall Country Park. The thirteen-year-old's father was planning to decorate her room and he had promised to do it to her taste. Kayleigh, blonde, blue-eyed and extrovert, was a complete contrast to her older green-eyed sister Tamsin, who chose to dress funereally as a Goth, with pale make-up, heavy eyeliner, dark lipstick and a shock of thick murky-purple hair. Tamsin had 'gone gothic' at thirteen, which involved staying in her own room to brood over books on vampires and the occult. In the new house in West Derby, the first thing Tamsin did was paint the walls of her room matt-black. Her parents didn't approve, but agreed that she could go ahead if she did it herself. It was a lovely summer afternoon and she had almost finished transforming her room to her liking, when there was a tap on the door.

"What?" said Tamsin, tetchily.

"Come and have look at this, Tam," came Kayleigh's muffled voice.

"Can't you see I'm busy," Tamsin snapped, as she sat cross-legged, carefully painting the skirting boards with black gloss and so obliterating the last hint of brightness from the room.

But Kayleigh was used to her sister's rebuffs and her blonde head intruded into the dark crypt of Tamsin's bedroom. "Just come and look at this, it's really really weird," Kayleigh said, with urgency in her usually melodic voice.

"You're weird." With a merciless slap of the paintbrush Tamsin swatted a tiny mayfly that had landed on the newly glossed skirting board and become stuck to it. "I told you I'm busy, and anyway, who gave you permission to come barging into my room? Get out!" she said, without turning to face her.

"But this is really spooky, Tam … and it looks evil."

Without realising it, Kayleigh had chosen the one word designed to capture Tamsin's imagination and with a sigh Tamsin got up and went to see what she was going on about.

Well, if it was weirdness she was after, she was in luck. About five feet up, on the pale painted beige wall facing Kayleigh's bed, there was a small black 'thing' which, on closer inspection, looked like a sketch of a match-stalk man, with a perfectly round circle for a head, a simple straight line for the torso, and the usual four bent lines to represent the arms and legs. This tiny figure looked as if it had been sketched by a pen with a pin-thin tip, such as might be used by an architect, for the lines were finer than a hair. The figure was about a centimetre in height, and although it was minute, Kayleigh said someone must have just drawn it, because she hadn't noticed it earlier.

"Okay, so what's spooky about it?" said Tamsin, irritated at having been stopped from working just for that, and she pressed her forefinger on to the little man and rubbed hard, but the figure couldn't be rubbed out. She licked her fingertip and tried again, but he seemed to be sketched in permanent ink.

"Just watch it closely for a minute," Kayleigh said.

"Why should I?" Tamsin's patience was growing thinner by the minute.

"Just watch, it's really freaky."

Kayleigh concentrated intently on the miniature match-stick man, but Tamsin only sighed and looked at it with one raised cynical eyebrow. It seemed to move slightly and its legs straightened up slightly, only by millimetres, but the movement was unmistakable. Tamsin was taken aback and swore with surprise. Her dark green eyes widened, and she backed away from the wall.

"Did you see that then? Did you see it move?" Kayleigh asked excitedly.

"Yeah, be quiet. What the hell is it?"

Tamsin was hooked. She stared intently at the little wire-frame man and now his arm seemed to rise up slightly. She backed away a little bit more and Kayleigh ran off to fetch her mother, Bess, but when she came upstairs to look at the little man he stayed resolutely still.

"I think you two should start getting a life," Bess told her daughters.

"Oh, mother, don't start," groaned Tamsin, and headed out of the room. "I'm off," she added, and left.

"Mum, just stand there and look at it for a bit, and you'll see it moves."

Kayleigh tried her utmost to make her mother believe what she and Tamsin had seen. "Honest, Mum, it's really weird, and our Tammy saw it too."

"Look, I've got things to do, Kay, like washing and cleaning and cooking. What're you going to do now anyway? Go on Facebook all day?"

Kayleigh gave up and folded her arms in a sulk and plonked herself down on the bed as her mother left the room. A little later she heard her arguing with her father downstairs as he returned from an outing from the local DIY store.

That night, Kayleigh lay in her bed, reading *Breakfast at Tiffany's* by the light of the bedside lamp, but ever mindful of the little man etched on the wall. She tried to concentrate but her eyes kept being drawn upwards towards him. At 1.20am, Kayleigh was still awake, but the words in the paperback seemed to be getting blurred, and her eyelids felt heavy. She folded down a corner of the page to mark her place, and just before she was ready to go to sleep, she went to have one last look. This time the little man was dancing!

Kayleigh doesn't recall opening the door and running out of the room. She just about remembers being in her parent's bedroom and waking her father up. Her dad, Mark, was rather annoyed, because he had to be up early in the morning for work. Kayleigh dragged him out of bed and pushed him into her bedroom, and switched on the main light.

"Dad, look!" she cried.

But the matchstick man had gone. Not a trace of him was there to be seen.

"Look, I've got to get to up early in the ..."

Kayleigh interrupted him, "It's gone! I don't believe it! It was here a minute ago and it was dancing."

"No, I don't believe it either," her father told her, looking at the blank wall. "You've had a nightmare, now get back to bed."

Mark then left the bedroom muttering to himself, and met his wife on the landing.

"What's up now?" Bess asked.

"She's had a bit of a nightmare, nothing to worry about," and walked past her to the toilet.

"It's that *Haunted Houses* programme she watches and all the rubbish she reads in those ghost books ... it plays on her mind."

When her parents had settled down, Kayleigh examined the spot where the little man had been on the wall, then crept into Tamsin's bedroom. Tamsin was lying face down in her bed, her black duvet on the floor. A solitary tea-light candle flickered in an oil burner on a circular table next to the bed. Next to the burner there was a photo of her ex-boyfriend, Russell, with pins stuck in his eyes.

"Tam, can I sleep with you tonight?" Kayleigh

whispered. There was not even a grunt of reply. "Something really odd has just happened in my room," Kayleigh told her. Still no reply. Kayleigh gently took hold of the duvet and lay down on the bed. At 3am Tamsin woke up and told her sister to go and sleep in her own room because she was "stinking the place out" with the pathetic deodorant she wore. Kayleigh went back to her own bedroom, and somehow managed to drift off into an uneasy state of light sleep.

Two days later, Kayleigh's room was decorated in the wallpaper she'd especially chosen – rosy pink with cherries in a sort of 1950s design. Tamsin mocked the paper of course. Being small, Kayleigh's bedroom was decorated within a day, and her father stood back and proudly surveyed his handiwork. Kayleigh loved it, but that night, the matchstick man returned. This time he was found on the wall near the bedside lamp. Kayleigh gasped in horror when she saw him, but she suspected Tamsin of drawing the figure to frighten her. She marched into her sister's room to find it empty. Then she realised that Tamsin was sleeping over at the house of her friend Emma tonight and had been there since 8pm. That figure on the wall must have only appeared within the last hour. Kayleigh went all cold inside.

Kayleigh wouldn't dare look close at the rudimentary depiction of a man in case it moved or danced. She placed a picture of her idol Audrey Hepburn over it and just hoped her father wouldn't see it. She lay on the other side of the bed, as far from that accursed matchstick mystery as possible, and she tried to read her book, but her thoughts naturally kept wandering back to the phantom sketcher. Who or what was drawing those little men on her wall and why? At half-past midnight, Kayleigh's dad called at her room and asked her if everything was okay. "Everything's peachy, thanks," she told him, but then he noticed the picture of Audrey Hepburn hanging on the wall near the headboard. "Why have you put that there?" he asked.

"It looks good there, by the lamp," Kayleigh replied, and blinked once – something she always did when she told a lie.

Her dad noticed it was crooked, and walked towards it to straighten it.

"Dad it's okay, just leave it please."

"What did you use, tacks or a nail?" he asked, reaching for the picture and lifting it off the wall.

There was no matchstick man behind it and Kayleigh shot a puzzled look at her father.

"It'd look better a bit higher up," said Mark, trying it a few feet above its original position. He babbled on about "the art of mounting pictures" but Kayleigh didn't take in a word of it – she was too ruffled by the disappearance of the match-stalk man.

On the following morning, in the shower, the teenager was rubbing shower gel into her arms when she happened to look down. There was a dark spot on her knee. She bent to look at it and felt her head swirl. It was the matchstick man. She tried to scrub it off with her mother's 'scrunchie' – a net body-puff loofah thing that hung in the shower cubicle, but the figure was as resistant as a tattoo.

Kayleigh showed the figure to her mother, who started to wonder if her daughter had drawn it on herself for attention, or some act of self-harm. Her father thought the same, but then something happened which showed the family that something genuinely unexplained was going on in Kayleigh's bedroom; more and more matchstick men appeared all over the new wallpaper. Bess made the sign of the cross when she saw two of the tiny figures appear on her daughter's large globular light shade. They looked like squirming insects until they looked close, and then they all saw that the wriggling black shapes were actually matchstick men doing some sort of odd dance. A sceptical neighbour was brought in, and she too witnessed the strange spectacle.

Hoping to find out about the house's previous owners, Mark paid a visit to the estate agent who had first shown him around the semi-detached property and talked him into buying it, and the agent seemed very uneasy, as if he had known the house had a strange history, but he pretended to be amused by the whole affair and said the previous owner of the house was an old woman who had moved down south. Grace, one of their elderly neighbours, was able to tell Mark that a woman in her seventies, who she had only known as Mrs Greer, had once lived at the house, and in the middle of the conversation, Grace suddenly gave a faint smile, then said something that knocked Mark for a six: "You've seen the little men haven't you?"

Mark nodded, and said that swarms of them were now appearing all over the house. Grace told him that she'd heard about the little matchstick men at the house in the 1970s. Mrs Greer used to see them, and the more she tried to erase them, the more they would appear, but if she didn't pay them any heed, they would gradually vanish. There was a story about the house Grace had heard, which dated back to the 1960s. A man in his twenties with a low mental age used to draw the figures on the walls of his bedroom at the house, and was sadistically beaten as a result by his strict and eccentric father. The lad fell and died in the bathroom during one beating, splitting his head open on the bath. Not long afterwards, the little men the young man had continually scrawled started to appear all over the walls of his room. That room, Mark discovered, was now Kayleigh's bedroom.

Mark told his wife and daughters to pay no heed to the matchstick men, or even talk about them. Nevertheless, one of the little men appeared on his wife's neck one evening soon after, but in a mammoth effort of willpower, she managed to ignore it. About a week later, the matchstick men faded, and they haven't been seen since.